Cambridge Elements

Elements in Gender and Politics
edited by
Tiffany D. Barnes
University of Texas at Austin
Diana Z. O'Brien
Washington University in St. Louis

FAMILY MATTERS

How Romantic Partners Shape Politicians' Careers

Johanna Rickne
Stockholm University

Olle Folke
Uppsala University

Moa Frödin Gruneau
University of Gothenburg

CAMBRIDGE
UNIVERSITY PRESS

Shaftesbury Road, Cambridge CB2 8EA, United Kingdom

One Liberty Plaza, 20th Floor, New York, NY 10006, USA

477 Williamstown Road, Port Melbourne, VIC 3207, Australia

314–321, 3rd Floor, Plot 3, Splendor Forum, Jasola District Centre, New Delhi – 110025, India

103 Penang Road, #05–06/07, Visioncrest Commercial, Singapore 238467

Cambridge University Press is part of Cambridge University Press & Assessment, a department of the University of Cambridge.

We share the University's mission to contribute to society through the pursuit of education, learning and research at the highest international levels of excellence.

www.cambridge.org
Information on this title: www.cambridge.org/9781009500623
DOI: 10.1017/9781009437837

© Johanna Rickne, Olle Folke and Moa Frödin Gruneau 2025

This publication is in copyright. Subject to statutory exception and to the provisions of relevant collective licensing agreements, with the exception of the Creative Commons version the link for which is provided below, no reproduction of any part may take place without the written permission of Cambridge University Press & Assessment.

An online version of this work is published at doi.org/10.1017/9781009437837 under a Creative Commons Open Access license CC-BY-NC 4.0 which permits re-use, distribution and reproduction in any medium for non-commercial purposes providing appropriate credit to the original work is given and any changes made are indicated. To view a copy of this license visit https://creativecommons.org/licenses/by-nc/4.0

When citing this work, please include a reference to the DOI 10.1017/9781009437837

First published 2025

A catalogue record for this publication is available from the British Library

ISBN 978-1-009-50062-3 Hardback
ISBN 978-1-009-43782-0 Paperback
ISSN 2753-8117 (online)
ISSN 2753-8109 (print)

Cambridge University Press & Assessment has no responsibility for the persistence or accuracy of URLs for external or third-party internet websites referred to in this publication and does not guarantee that any content on such websites is, or will remain, accurate or appropriate.

Family Matters

How Romantic Partners Shape Politicians' Careers

Elements in Gender and Politics

DOI: 10.1017/9781009437837
First published online: March 2025

Johanna Rickne
Stockholm University

Olle Folke
Uppsala University

Moa Frödin Gruneau
University of Gothenburg

Author for correspondence: Moa Frödin Gruneau, moa.frodin.gruneau@gu.se

Abstract: This Element studies how career support from romantic partners affects career patterns and costs in politics. It argues that a lower level of career support from romantic partners leads to a lower likelihood for political promotion among women politicians (the partner support hypothesis), as well as greater stress on women politicians' relationships when they advance (the career stress hypothesis). Both predictions find support in Swedish data for more than 80,000 political careers over a fifty-year period. Women politicians are in relationships that prioritize their male partner's career and where that partner does less unpaid work in the household. This is important in explaining women's career disadvantage. It also explains why promotions double the divorce rate for women but leave men's relationships intact. The analysis sheds light on the role played by romantic partners in gender inequality in politics. This title is also available as Open Access on Cambridge Core.

Keywords: Gender inequality, Romantic partner, Political careers, Divorce, Children.

© Johanna Rickne, Olle Folke and Moa Frödin Gruneau 2025

ISBNs: 9781009500623 (HB), 9781009437820 (PB), 9781009437837 (OC)
ISSNs: 2753-8117 (online), 2753-8109 (print)

Contents

1 Introduction — 1

2 Romantic Partners and Politicians' Career Advancement — 3

3 Gender Gaps in Political Career Advancement — 14

4 Politicians' Romantic Relationships — 22

5 Romantic Partners as a Source of Career Inequality — 30

6 Political Promotions and Relationship Stress — 40

7 Conclusions and Discussion: Where Do We Go Now? — 49

References — 54

1 Introduction

Memoirs of successful politicians often contain stories about their romantic partners. When Ron de Santis started his political career in Florida by campaigning for the U.S. House, his wife Casey knocked on "thousands of doors" and was, he wrote, instrumental to his victory. This narrative contrasts with U.S. vice presidential nominee Sarah Palin's story of her early campaigning in Wasilla, Alaska, where she prodded along from door to door on her own, dragging along two children in a sled. This is not only an American phenomenon. The Swedish politician Birgitta Ohlsson (2017) writes that her political career wouldn't have been possible without her husband's support. She also advises other women to choose their life partners with the utmost care, emphasizing that partner support is crucial not only for day-to-day household matters but also for respect for one's ideas and emotional support.

This Element discusses how romantic partners shape politicians' careers. We describe how they can be either a support system for advancement or a source of challenges and frictions. This study illuminates how, like the stories of Ron De Santis and Sarah Palin illustrate, the roles played by the romantic partner differ in important ways between women and men in politics.

Section 2 develops a theoretical framework for understanding the dual roles of romantic partners. This framework combines economic theory on the division of work within households, political science theory on political career advancement, and sociological theory on gender norms. It predicts that women politicians receive less career support from their partners than men, and that this helps explain their slower political career advancement. It also predicts that the romantic partner becomes a greater source of stress and tension when women politicians advance in their career. This stress generates trade-offs between a stable family life and a career in politics; thus career advancement may come at a steeper personal price for women.

By focusing on romantic partners, this study enhances our understanding of gender inequalities in politics and in the economy more broadly. In the majority of countries, women are underrepresented in most positions of power in most sectors. They advance more slowly in their careers than men and often do not reach as far. Women still make up little more than 25 percent of parliamentarians around the world (www.ipu.org), fewer than 10 percent of Fortune 500 CEOs (www.fortune.com), and less than a third of tenured university professors (www.ec.europa.eu). These career disparities reduce women's economic resources, status, and voice in society relative to men and undermine aggregate economic growth and human rights at the societal level (e.g., Hsieh et al., 2019).

Past studies have uncovered many reasons why women advance more slowly in their careers. Romantic partners have formed an integral part of this research agenda, but a lack of detailed data has made it difficult to empirically study their effects on career advancement over time. We overcome this problem by compiling a comprehensive and detailed dataset on Swedish politicians and their partners. We investigate how nearly 80,000 politicians' careers advance (or not) over a period of fifty years and link this information to traits of the partnership. Detailed administrative records kept by the Swedish government let us measure politicians' civil status in yearly data and characterize the degree of partner support using data on paid work from tax records and unpaid work from social insurance records.

Women and men are more economically and socially equal in Sweden than in most countries, including in politics. During our fifty-year study period, the proportion of women in elected local and national office rose to nearly 50 percent, partly due to gender quotas adopted by some political parties. Yet substantial inequalities remain even in this context. For example, women hold a minority of the powerful *appointed* political positions in Sweden. We also demonstrate that political career advancement places a substantially higher personal cost on women than men by creating more stress and tension in their romantic relationships. Observing these gender differences even in a setting of substantial equality and commitment to gender egalitarian norms suggests they are likely to apply elsewhere as well.

Combining a career and family is easier in Sweden than in most other countries. Government-funded universal childcare and elder care have outsourced much of the care work formerly undertaken by women in the household to the public sector. Replacing family-based taxation with individual taxation has incentivized dual-earner households, and the extensive parental leave system is especially generous to those with labor market attachment prior to parenthood, incentivizing families to increase women's labor force participation. These policies have reduced the trade-offs between career and family as far back as the 1970s. They likely help explain why we do not observe a large gender gap in the likelihood that politicians have romantic partners, which mirrors the gap in other countries (Joshi and Goehrung, 2021). This margin of friction, that is, a greater need for women to choose between pursuing a career and having a romantic partner, will undoubtedly be more important in other contexts where progress toward building institutions that favor gender inequality in the labor market have not progressed as far.

Our study offers new insights into how romantic partners influence gender equality in politics. We explain how partners can offer unique emotional and practical support to people who want to invest the considerable time and energy needed to pursue higher political office – or cause friction and stress rather than ambition and drive. We highlight how the persistent strong gender norms for couple formation hamper women's economic and political empowerment. Couple formation and the division of household responsibilities have progressed more slowly toward gender equality compared to expectations and behaviors in the labor market. Thus women generally lack the type of supportive relationships that facilitate climbing to the top of a career ladder in any sector. While we show that this is true for the politics sector, our insights apply throughout the economy.

This Element proceeds as follows. In Section 2 we introduce a theoretical framework for understanding how romantic partners influence politicians' career advancement. In Section 3, we describe our data, discuss the relevant political institutions, and provide an empirical overview of the gender gap in career progression. Section 4 describes how career support from romantic relationships is different for men and women politicians. In Section 5 we establish that romantic relationships can help explain gender differences in career advancement. Section 6 demonstrates how promotions can put stress and strain on romantic relationships – especially for women politicians.

2 Romantic Partners and Politicians' Career Advancement

Just as in a private sector organization, politicians start at a lower level and advance over time as they learn the job and develop their leadership potential. Political careers usually start in less prestigious local political offices and progress to more powerful offices. Most politicians climb the rungs of the political career ladder by accumulating work experience (seniority) and skills, and expanding their networks. In a comparative study of eight European countries, Cotta and Best (2007) observed that a substantial majority of members of parliament, in some cases reaching 90 percent, started as local politicians. Local politics is a common pathway to national political office in the United States as well (Anzia and Bernhard, 2022). We calculate that approximately two-thirds of Swedish parliamentarians previously held an elected office at the local level.

Several actors jointly determine this upward advancement in politics. Norris and Lovenduski's (1995) "supply and demand" model categorizes actors as either supplying certain people for higher office or demanding certain people for those positions. The demand side consists of voters and parties who select officeholders from a group of willing candidates. Individuals who are willing to serve constitute the supply side. Upward advancement is the result of an interplay between the three groups.

A country's electoral system shapes the relative importance of voters, parties, and politicians in determining advancement. Voters play a more important role in majoritarian systems, where politicians compete against each other individually. Parties play a more important role in proportional representation systems, such as in Sweden, where voters select parties rather than individuals and only candidates near the top of the party's ballot have a chance of being elected. Individual politicians are important regardless of the electoral system and, we argue, so are their romantic partners.

The Romantic Partner as a Career Resource or Constraint

Economic models of the family provide a useful starting point for understanding how a romantic partner shapes a person's career (Reid, 1934; Becker, 1981). These theories conceptualize the household as a small business with two workers who collaborate to maximize their lifestyle. Both partners want to consume and have a home where they can enjoy that consumption and their leisure time. This requires allocating both partners' time to paid work in the labor market and unpaid work in the household. Time allocated to paid labor brings in the money needed for consumption (e.g., buying the ingredients for a meal) and time devoted to household work lets them enjoy this consumption (cooking and eating the meal). The household needs to dedicate time to both spheres to ensure a fulfilling life. In these models, children are a public good in the theoretical sense that both parents enjoy them.

Such models emphasize the theoretical concept of incentives for specialization. Couples may organize their time so that one person "specializes" in market work and the other in household work based on assumptions about productivity growth as a person spends more time on a certain type of task. More time spent in paid work raises the person's productivity as they learn on the job and advance up the career ladder. Their hourly pay increases and gives the household more money for consumption per unit of time. This increases total production more than investing equal time in both partners' careers.

According to such household models, a romantic partner either helps or hinders a person's career progression. Because households decide jointly how to allocate their time, a couple's career decisions become linked. A fulfilling life requires time allocated to both labor market and household work, and one person's time in the market requires the other's work in the household to maintain both partners' quality of life. The incentive to specialize causes the household to prioritize one person's career over that of the other. The partner with the higher income is in a better bargaining position to negotiate a lower share of the household work (Lundberg and Pollak, 1993). The partner who specializes in the household provides the necessary "ground service" that allows their partner's career to take flight, but sacrifices their own career over time and cannot expect this time allocation to flip (Becker, 1973, 1974).

Specialization sometimes leads one partner to work outside the home while the other spends all their time on household tasks. For example, Prillaman (2023) convincingly argues that married women in rural India are subordinated to men within the household, which limits their political agency and opportunities for political engagement. The specialization between home and market work is often less extreme in Western countries. Iversen and Rosenbluth (2006) explain that dual-earner households are common despite the strong incentives for specialization because marriage is an incomplete contract. Men and women are both motivated to participate in paid work as it enhances their alternatives outside the marriage; it also increases women's chances of favorable outcomes if they divorce and boosts their bargaining power within the marriage.

There are also gendered patterns to how paid work is organized in dual-earner households, which need to flexibly allocate time to household work. One partner (more often the woman) can pursue work with fewer hours and/or more time flexibility, but this is costly for a person's career, especially in highly paid and prestigious professions (Goldin, 2014) where the employer expects flexibility and long working hours from their employees.

While economic theory explains households' incentives to specialize, it does not convincingly justify why this specialization is usually gender based. Most heterosexual households prioritize the husband's career while the wife dedicates more of her time to the household.[1] Becker's original theory did not address this discrepancy, but briefly referenced pregnancy and breastfeeding as women's initial comparative (biological) advantage within the household. They proposed that even a small advantage of this kind could, over time, result in a large productivity gap as each spouse experiences productivity growth in their chosen sphere of work. A more plausible explanation for the gender-based specialization in paid versus unpaid work is the strong social norms regarding women's and men's behaviors in couple formation and time allocation (Eagly, 1987; West and Zimmerman 1987; Eagly and Wood, 2012). Studies of gender inequality in the labor market reveal the importance of gender norms for labor market outcomes. For example, parenthood is often a starting point for differences in earnings between men and women. The gender earnings gap is much

---

[1] Theories about how specialization is gendered mainly apply to different-sex couples. We do not theorize about whether our framework could be applied to same-sex couples. Our sample contains very few same-sex couples, so studying them separately is not possible; our analysis therefore includes all couples.

more pronounced in countries with more conservative gender norms (Kleven et al., 2019).

The political science literature sometimes assumes that gender equality in political representation will be automatically achieved when women and men become more economically equal (Sapiro, 1982; Burns et al., 2001). Yet such research overlooks the role of couple formation. Norms on couple formation encourage families to engage in gender-based specialization. The social expectation that women should "marry up" and men should "marry down" results in most couples forming between a younger woman and an older, more professionally accomplished man. Social norms driving this inequality are clearly visible in popular culture, such as the notion that women should look for the prince in a fairytale or a medical doctor who represents a "good catch." Society enforces these norms: when a husband is successful in the labor market, the wife is said to "shine" too, but if the wife is more successful people ask, "Who is wearing the pants in this relationship?" Even though people tend to pair up with someone from the same social class, there is considerable inequality between the two partners in nearly every culture, including in Scandinavia and Sweden (e.g., Boschini et al., 2011; Almås et al., 2023).

Because couples start off on unequal footing, initial comparative advantages may result in gender-based specialization. The older partner might have advanced further in their career and earn a higher salary. Their age alone gives them the upper hand in joint decision-making on whose career should take precedence. By looking for husbands with a higher economic status than their own, women are putting themselves at a disadvantage in later reallocations of the household's time and thus struggle to prioritize their own careers. In countries where most politicians come from certain highly paid "pipeline professions," strong norms for unequal couple formation also exist in the most economically strong groups. Even in relatively recent graduate cohorts from top American business schools, most women expect their husband's career to take precedence in their (future) household, and an even larger proportion find themselves in this situation once they find that partner (Ely et al., 2014). In sum, even if women and men are equally economically strong early in life, if current norms for couple formation persist, gender inequality in the labor market and politics will emerge when couples form. This is the case for all social groups, including the most well-off and the most likely political candidates.

A second type of gender norm that causes gender-based specialization in the household consists of beliefs about women's and men's skills and talents. Social expectations ascribe the role of breadwinner to men and the role of caretaker to women. Men are believed to have the traits needed for high-paying careers, such as intelligence, competitiveness, and risk taking (the phenomenon of "think manager, think male," Schein, 1973; Schein et al., 1996). Women are thought to be good at care activities and emotionally connecting with others. These norms have weakened since Betty Friedan wrote *The Feminine Mystique* in 1963, and women's career ambitions are no longer characterized as a psychological pathology based in "penis envy" or by women's mental and emotional inability to work for pay. Yet these ideas are reflected in phenomena such as the "bell curve hypothesis," which ascribes men's overrepresentation in high-paying jobs to an overrepresentation in the upper tail of the intelligence distribution (as Larry Summers famously argued to explain the underrepresentation of women among Harvard faculty members). Nearly half the world's population believe men make better political leaders than women do – more than twice the size of the gender bias against women business leaders (UNDP, 2023).

Gender-specific beliefs about women's and men's skills and talents generate perceptions about their productivity in the home and labor market. For example, a conviction that the man will be more productive in the labor market and the woman in the household makes it rational for her to dedicate her time to lowering the costs of his career by spending her own time and efforts on mental and practical household labor.

How Partners Provide Specific Resources to Support Political Careers

Political science theory provides detailed insights into the individual resources that help a person enter and advance in politics. Romantic relationships help explain how individuals accumulate these resources. Both partners' time, money, skills, and ambitions are interconnected and affected by the division of labor between workforce and household responsibilities. In this section we discuss the significance of time, money, skills, and ambition in shaping political careers, and how having a supportive partner helps an individual acquire these resources.

Time is a key resource for any form of political participation (Verba and Nie, 1972; Brady et al., 1995). Political party members and campaign activists need to attend meetings and mobilize voters in their free time. Wylie (2018) describes political positions in Brazil as a "third shift" that individuals engage in after their "first shift" in the labor market and "second shift" in the household. A romantic partner can ease these time constraints for the politician by allocating less time to paid work and more time to household responsibilities; this becomes especially important as their political career progresses and they transition from unpaid to paid political positions. Top political jobs usually have long inflexible work hours and require the individual's physical presence, which increases the need for partner support (following theory by, e.g., Goldin and Katz, 2011; Goldin, 2014). The work is multifaceted and requires politicians to balance the tasks of their office, the tasks within the party organizations, and multiple demands from the media, voters, and interest groups. Their work often spills over to evenings and weekends. The nature of the workflow is also unpredictable: politicians need to respond to political events and the general news cycle, which further increases the need for a romantic partner willing to flexibly adapt to these circumstances.

Money is an important resource for political advancement in some contexts (Verba and Nie, 1972). In the absence of public funds for political campaigns, individual politicians are responsible for paying more of the costs themselves. Women's lower earnings thus reduce their monetary resources and electoral chances in high-cost contexts such as Brazil or the United States (Wylie, 2018, recently reviewed by Grumbach et al., 2020). The near-complete absence of couple formations that strongly prioritize the woman's career clearly restrict the pool of women with sufficient earnings from their own careers. These restrictions may also indirectly prevent women from entering and advancing in demanding and inflexible occupations that help individuals develop strong donor networks, such as lawyers in the United States (Goldin, 2014; Bonica, 2020; Thomsen and King, 2020). Money is a less important resource in contexts such as Sweden, which has a party-centered electoral system and public campaign finance.

Civic and practical *skills* constitute another resource for political career advancement (Verba and Nie, 1972; Besley, 2006). These resources include speaking and writing skills, as well as organizational skills in leading meetings and managing groups. The latter becomes increasingly important when advancing in politics, because political leadership involves coordinating various activities and a multiple types of communication. While educational settings and the household help individuals learn some of these skills, paid work provides more experience. People with less work experience and less demanding careers therefore find it harder to accumulate the necessary skills to advance in their careers. Women in couples who prioritize the husband's career will not accumulate these skills at the same rate as men. In other words, to maximize the skills needed for a political career, women need a partner who is supportive of their career. Unlike other highly paid professions, political jobs do not have dedicated educational programs; they rely heavily on on-the-job training. Yet women without partner support have less time to learn on the job.

Career *ambitions* are necessary for advancement in any job. Past research has documented that women are less willing than men to advance to higher rungs on the career ladder (e.g., Bledsoe and Herring, 1990; Fulton et al., 2006;

Allen, 2013). Others find no gap, such as Folke and Rickne (2016). Advancing in politics may require women to be more ambitious than their male counterparts, given negative views of women's competence, the male dominance of the political sector, and the time constraints associated with political careers (Palmer and Simon, 2003; Bos et al., 2022). Advancing in a political career involves replacing one's previous labor market career with a political career, which becomes a full-time job. Because most women work in stereotypically "women's" occupations and women-dominated workplaces, this switch will require more political ambition than for men, who may be more mentally acclimatized and feel comfortable in these male-dominated settings. Similarly, men are more likely to work in jobs with little time flexibility, while women more often have jobs with greater time flexibility. If replacing one's career with a political career is a larger change of work conditions for women than for men, this too requires more political ambition from women. In sum, the gendered aspects of highly paid prestigious jobs are important for political careers in two ways. First, political careers generally have low time flexibility. Second, since women are more likely to have a partner with a low-flexibility job, if a woman pursues a political career this represents a greater challenge to the household's previous time allocation.

The role of family obligations in creating the gender gap in career ambitions has been the subject of some debate. While some influential studies maintain that family obligations do not represent a significant obstacle to *entering* politics (Fox and Lawless, 2014), many more find strong support for the idea that women's family dynamics depress their progressive ambition. For example, married women have lower progressive ambition in U.S. politics compared to single women (Fulton et al., 2006) and women self-report that family costs (such as separation from family and friends) put them off advancing (Maestas et al., 2006). Within elite groups in society, politically ambitious women and men have very similar traits (Fox and Lawless, 2010). Among ordinary citizens, however, there are gendered patterns of political ambition. In general, marriage is beneficial for men's political ambitions, but not for women's (Crowder-Meyer, 2020): there are sharp differences between partner support in the average marriage for men versus the average marriage for women. The gender difference in the utility of marriage is likely because in dual-earner households women tend to do a larger share of the housework (Hochschild, 1989), and this double shift constrains their leisure time (Bernhard et al., 2021). As many political careers start in unpaid local political office, having the time to invest in such roles is key to political ambition. A crucial theoretical insight in this literature is that a person's career ambitions are a function of their social relationships with external actors, including their partner

(Carroll and Sanbonmatsu, 2013; Bernhard et al., 2021). A supportive partner will not only free up time for them to pursue their career; they will also offer support by celebrating the good times and helping them navigate the hard times. Career ambitions are more likely to thrive if a romantic partner is supportive of one's career.

Voters and Parties

The previous sections largely discussed a politician's career advancement as a function of how their own resources are determined in interplay with a romantic partner. We now examine the two other actors in the selection process—voters and parties—to discuss how romantic partners may directly or indirectly shape their choices among the available political candidates.

There is some evidence that voters might prefer politicians who have spouses and children to those who do not (see, e.g., Teele et al., 2018). A politician's romantic partnership may therefore help them get elected, especially if the partner actively participates in their campaign. This mechanism can operate in contexts where politicians' family situations are known to the public and shape its voting behavior and/or where parties believe voters will know and care about politicians' family circumstances. It will matter less in contexts like Sweden, where politicians' family situations are generally unknown to the public and family members rarely or never appear in political campaigns.

Parties play a more important role in electing individual politicians in the Swedish system. A 2002 reform introduced preference votes, but very few candidates received enough to clear the high threshold. Even if preference votes affect future leadership appointments by indicating which politician is the most popular (Folke et al., 2016), only 1 percent of those elected based on preference vote support. Parties help determine advancement up the political hierarchy by nominating politicians for higher office or appointing them to influential positions after they are elected. Candidates are nominated in Sweden in a variety of ways; in some parties, party leaders make these decisions, while in others, the process is less centralized and members (or sometimes even voters) participate in internal primaries. As in any other career, building internal support to get promoted requires doing one's job well and cultivating support from leaders and colleagues. As the previous section described, a politician's romantic partner will affect how much time they can devote to such tasks and their level of ambition to perform them. This process of building skills and networks takes place over time: politicians spend year after year in their collective efforts to make policy and administer various sectors and government functions under their control.

Women may need a greater level of support from their romantic partner to obtain the same promotion chances as their male counterparts within the party structure. This is because those structures may hold women to a higher standard, for example, via homosocial recruitment where male leaders prefer male followers (Besley et al., 2017). Evidence abounds that parties put women at a disadvantage. They are less active in recruiting women to run (e.g., Niven, 1998; Fox and Lawless, 2010) and may systematically recruit women for unwinnable seats or low ballot ranks (Krook, 2010; Esteve-Volart and Bagues, 2012; Thomas and Bodet, 2013). Feminist institutionalism stresses how internal party rules and norms that appear gender neutral may disadvantage women (Krook and Mackay, 2011). This could include work conditions that are less family friendly, such as meetings late in the day or on weekends, or seniority rules that make it harder for political newcomers (who are more likely to be women) to advance (van Dijk, 2023).

Children

The arrival of children often triggers an increase in gender-based specialization within the household (Lundberg and Rose, 2000; Budig and England, 2001). Parenthood adds new time demands on the couple, and these tasks are stereotypically viewed as more suitable for women. Social expectations that women take on this work mean that parenthood often triggers a less equal division of household labor and makes parents re-evaluate their labor market choices in ways that are influenced by these gender norms (Hochschild, 1989). Women take longer parental leave and reduce their work hours after becoming mothers, or sometimes quit the labor force completely, while fathers generally continue without much change. One source of these social expectations is the organization where the woman is employed, which may consider mothers less productive and deserving of career advancement (Hideg et al., 2018; Kitroeff and Silver-Greenberg, 2018).

Even in households where incomes are high enough to allow substantial outsourcing of tasks related to parenthood, the burden tends to be unequally shared. There is little evidence that comparative advantage applies even in households where the wife earns more and should arguably have an advantage in paid labor (Bittman et al., 2003; England et al., 2016). And even in couples with the large economic resources required to outsource domestic work, women assume a larger mental burden in organizing these, as well as other aspects of the child's life (Reich-Stiebert et al., 2023). Having children requires planning and organizing various activities (hobbies, clothes, food, friends, homework, etc.) and this cognitive load may weigh more heavily on women's political engagement (Weeks, 2022). The share of households that consist of high-earning, two-income couples has increased alongside recent changes in norms about parenting. Norms about active involvement in childcare are common in well-off families (Craig et al., 2014). Such norms likely contribute to parents being reluctant to outsource many of the childcare responsibilities even when they have the economic means.

Research on politicians has uncovered several important patterns in their family structures. Women politicians are less likely to be parents and tend to have fewer children than men politicians (Dodson, 1997; Campbell and Childs, 2014; Thomas and Bittner, 2017; Joshi and Goehrung, 2021). Other studies have concluded that children have a larger negative impact on women's progressive political ambitions (Fulton et al., 2006).

A key reason that children might play a less important role in gender gaps in political careers relative to other sectors is that such careers usually start later in life. Rather than beginning after high school or university, political careers start later and develop alongside the person's regular employment. So, while the arrival of children might crowd out the time available for taking on the "third shift," thereby disrupting early career phases, politicians generally switch to full-time political after the early, more time-intensive period of parenthood. The *arrival of children* is therefore less likely to trigger an expanded career gap for a meaningful proportion of politicians for the simple reason that most people are already parents by the time they seek to make this switch. For these upward moves, the division of time regarding parenting duties nevertheless matters because it creates differential resources for political career progression.

Stress and Friction in the Relationship

As sociological research predicts, if women receive less career support from their romantic partners than men, this will likely produce more stress and strain in their relationships as their political career develops. This literature has claimed that critical transition points in a person's career (i.e., promotions or demotions) can cause particularly high levels of tension if a promotion triggers a renegotiation of the spouses' roles in the household and in the paid labor market (e.g., Coverman, 1989). Such renegotiation, or "role cycling," could be more common in promoted women's relationships than in men's, since the women initially took on a greater share of household responsibilities.

According to key works in family economics, labor market events that change the performance of spouses in relation to what was expected at the time of couple formation may shift the balance of utility from the marriage versus the utility of being single. Because most relationships specialize around the husband's career from the outset, his later career success is more likely to conform with these expectations, while the wife's success contradicts them (e.g., Becker et al., 1977; Weiss and Willis, 1997). While these frameworks consider divorce to be a rational outcome of the costs and benefits of remaining married, its stressfulness and ill effects on health have been well established (reviewed by Amato, 2010). While certain couples may be predisposed to both divorce and experiencing stress, Amato (2010) finds that divorce generally heightens tension between partners. However, divorce can also have positive outcomes, for instance if a woman relies on promotions for financial independence and divorce marks the conclusion of a dysfunctional and stressful relationship. However, this optimistic scenario is unlikely to apply to political promotions to top positions, as most Swedish politicians already earn high salaries before advancing in their careers (Folke and Rickne, 2020).

Empirical Predictions to Take to the Data

Based on our theoretical discussion, we derive two predictions about how romantic partners shape gender differences in politicians' careers. The first concerns whether partners function as a career support or a career constraint. As we discuss in this section, men are more often in relationships in which both partners' time allocations focus on promoting his career success. Women are often in the opposite situation (their husband's career takes priority) or the prioritization may be balanced more equally between the two partners. We therefore derive the **Career support hypothesis**: *Women's lower level of career support from romantic partners can help explain their slower advancement in politics.*

In an empirical extension, we predict that *children will exacerbate the need for career support from the partner and increase the level of inequality.*

Our second prediction concerns the strain placed on a relationship if one of the partners advances in their career. We expect women to face more tension in their relationship after a promotion due to lower career support from their partner. We predict that *upward career moves cause more stress on the average woman's relationship*. We study whether women's advancement in politics is more likely to result in divorce.

This section has combined theories from multiple academic disciplines to describe how romantic partners may shape a politician's career advancement. Based on this framework, we derived two predictions about how these influences lead to unequal career advancement for women and men: (1) partners provide more career support to men than to women politicians and thereby affect their likelihood of advancing and (2) advancement puts different levels of stress on women's and men's relationships due to this variation in support. This second prediction does not anticipate differences in the *likelihood* of advancing but expects career advancement to come at a higher personal cost to women than to men.

We expect our predictions to hold across political parties. Parties determine the ranking of their candidates and thus play an important role in deciding their political career possibilities. Building internal support is key to promotion in all parties. A politician needs both time and ambition to acquire the skills and networks necessary to gain internal party support, and a politician's romantic partner will affect their time and ambition. Therefore, partner support should be crucially important to climbing the career ladder in all parties. We will include summaries of our main results across parties at the end of each section.

3 Gender Gaps in Political Career Advancement

This section investigates whether women and men advance up Sweden's political career ladder at the same speed. Sweden is a multiparty system with proportional representation; parties compete by offering slates of rank-ordered candidates. Synchronized elections take place every fourth year for municipalities (290), regions (20), and parliament.

The Swedish government has an hourglass structure across three administrative levels. Our analysis concentrates on the more politically powerful national and municipal levels; the regional level primarily focuses on health care. Municipalities have significant political autonomy and control budgets of 15–20 percent of the country's GDP. They employ around 20 percent of the labor force within their areas of political and administrative responsibility, such as childcare and elder care.

Most politicians start their career at the municipal level by becoming a party member and local activist. These roles involve, for example, going to party meetings and working on political campaigns and policies. All party members are eligible to appear on the electoral ballot. Each municipality is effectively a parliamentary system in microcosm; local branches of the national parties determine which candidates appear on the ballot, and in what order. The rank order of the ballot is crucial for getting elected, because seats are distributed from the top of the list of names. Municipal political party leaders usually appear at the top of the ballots (often referred to as the "top name" or *toppnamn* in Swedish).

After a municipal election, the majority party, or, most often, a majority coalition, forms the local government. This majority appoints the mayor, who serves as the chairperson of the local council board (typically the first-ranked politician of the largest party in the governing coalition). The mayorship is a full-time job with a wage in the top 5 percent of the Swedish wage distribution. Municipal councilors are unpaid; they continue to hold their regular jobs. They attend regular council meetings and receive a small lump-sum honorarium of around 20 USD. Roughly two-thirds of all first-time parliamentarians have previously been a municipal councilor. The parliament is, of course, more politically important than the average municipal assembly, but being the mayor of a large city is more politically important than being a newly elected parliamentarian.

We conceptualize a simple political career ladder with three rungs: local municipal councilor, local party leader (top name), and parliamentarian. We conduct a subsample analysis on top-ranked politicians in the largest party in the governing political majority to identify mayors. This approach captures key career steps and allows us to analyze all political parties with representation in parliament.[2]

In this section, and in Section 4, we explore gender differences in career advancement for all politicians regardless of their relationship status. We include both couples and singles in a first step to describe the political system and gender gaps in general before studying couples to determine how personal relationships can help us understand gender gaps in political advancement.

Data Sources

Swedish law requires political parties to submit their electoral ballots to the electoral authority and include the personal identification code of each politician. We digitize ballot papers back to the 1970s for parliamentarians and 1973 for municipal councilors, which generates a list of all elected politicians at the municipal and national levels. Information to identify local party leaders is sometimes missing, either because there is no information on list rank or because a party has several electoral ballots with different top names. We are therefore unable to identify the party leader in 48.5 percent of the municipality–party combinations before 1991, and 10 percent after.

We use two data sources to identify mayors. Between 1982 and 2006 we use the top-ranked politician on the ballot of the party that appointed the mayor.[3] Starting in 2006 we use information from a mandatory survey conducted by

---

[2] Previous research documents gender gaps in promotions to mid-level municipal government careers (namely chairs and vice chairs of political committees), which we do not study here (Folke and Rickne, 2016).

[3] Data on the party that appointed the mayor was obtained from the Kfakta database collected by Leif Johansson (Department of Political Science, University of Lund).

Statistics Sweden, which collects the personal identification codes of all mayors. Due to missing data for list rank and the existence of multiple ballots, we are unable to identify the mayor in about half of the municipalities prior to 1991 and 15 percent between 1991 and 2002.

The individual identification codes let us chart the career paths of 80,000 politicians over a fifty-year period. We can see when they first become a councilor, if they move up to become the local party leader in each election, and if they become a parliamentarian. Our sample does not include politicians representing local parties with no seats in parliament (fewer than 4 percent of municipal councilors).

To measure traits of the politicians and their partners, we merge the politician data with other administrative records at the year-person level using politicians' personal ID codes. These records are yearly panel data for all Swedish permanent residents (1968–2019). None are self-reported and all have very high accuracy and a small proportion of missing values. We use the government's variable for age and binary sex, which are encoded from an individual's personal identification number. Sex is recorded at birth but can be altered later if a person changes their sex. We lack any information about gender beyond this binary classification. The next section gives more details on the variables and datasets we use to study politicians' intra-household allocation of market and household work.

Institutions for Career Advancement

Candidate selection procedures are similar across parties in Swedish municipalities (for a detailed description, see Widenstjerna, 2020). At the local level, members and party branches such as clubs in neighborhoods and demographic groups (women's branch, youth league, etc.) nominate potential candidates. An election committee composed of senior party members prepares a shortlist and organizes a primary election among party members; the Social Democrats solicit candidate preferences from local branches instead. The committee uses these results to propose a final rank-ordered ballot, which a general party meeting usually approves without revisions.

Electoral lists for parliament are created in a very similar manner (for more detailed descriptions, see Johansson, 1999; Fransson, 2018). Election committees in each parliamentary constituency nominate and rank candidates before a decision on the final list is taken in a nomination meeting (*nominerinsstämma*). These committees, often comprised of prominent local party members, strongly influence which names appear on the list. Members can nominate candidates; some parties employ advisory internal primaries to determine which candidates have more support from party members.

Advancing within the party requires support from colleagues and senior politicians. No single person has control over the ballot ranking, but the local party leadership exerts an outsized influence via internal primaries and the nomination committee. Doing a good job and demonstrating ambition will help an individual advance, and group interactions during the election period within the party and in political office allow a politician's colleagues to observe their skills and competencies. Having the possibility to spend a lot of time and effort in the party organization and on one's appointment(s)—as well as getting to know the party, its people and policies—greatly helps a person build the internal support needed to advance.

As in Norway (Cirone et al., 2021), there is a strong seniority system in Sweden; politicians tend to climb higher on the electoral ballot over time. A person who wants to run again is rarely prevented from appearing on a ballot unless they have committed some type of wrongdoing. Politicians rarely fall in the ballot ranks, with the exception of consensual downward moves for politicians who retire in practice but continue to lend their name to the party ("list fillers").

Figure 1 illustrates that while seniority helps advancement, it is by no means the only promotion criterion; nor is it applied equally to women and men. The figure takes all municipal councilors elected after 1979 and plots the proportion of local party leaders by the number of previous election periods in the municipal council. It depicts a clear positive relationship between seniority and promotion among all parties (left) and the largest party in the governing majority (right). However, a sizable proportion of councilors with long tenures are not leaders, and it is possible to quickly become a leader.

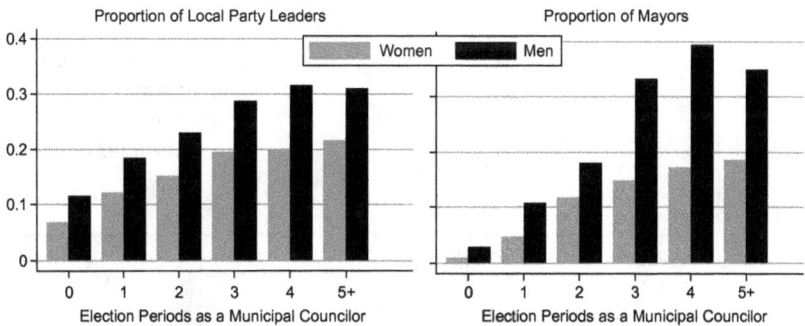

Figure 1 Seniority-based promotions to local party leadership.

Notes: The figure shows the share of politicians who are ranked first on their party's ballot in all parties (local party leader, left) and in the largest party in the governing majority (mayor, right). N (Women, left) = 37,120; N (Men, left) = 54,394; N (Women, right) = 21,736; N (Men, right) = 32,153.

Comparing the gray bars for women and the black bars for men reveals a large gender difference in the relationship between seniority and promotion. Among politicians with little or no seniority, men are more likely than women to have been promoted, and for each additional term of experience, men's probability of being a party leader increases more than women's. By three election periods, the gap is nearly 10 percentage points (or 30 percent) to men's advantage. While seniority helps both women and men advance, men's promotion probability grows more with seniority than women's. In additional analyses (not shown) we investigated seniority-based promotions over time and by party. The pattern is similar, but with a somewhat smaller gender gap in the most recent decades. We also observe a positive relationship between seniority and promotion probability for all parties.

Descriptive Representation on the Political Career Ladder

Figure 2 depicts the proportion of women on the four rungs of our political career ladder. It shows the proportion of women among all municipal councilors and parliamentarians and the proportion of local party leaders in municipality–party combinations where a party has five or more elected municipal councilors.

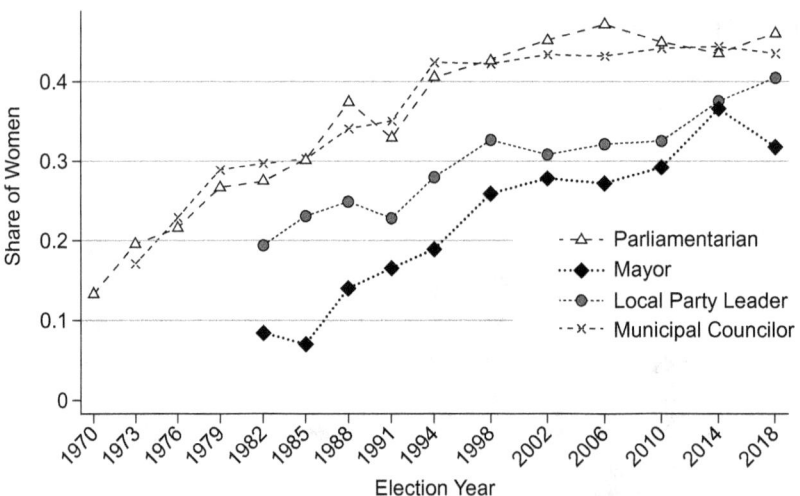

Figure 2 Share of women in political positions.

Notes: Data for municipal politics is restricted to political parties with representation in parliament (96 percent of all municipal politicians) and municipalities where the party has five or more elected councilors. N (Municipal councilors) = 186,910, N (Local party leader) = 8,235, N (Mayor) = 2,549, N (Parliamentarian) = 5,206.

These proportions of women have grown over time on three career levels, but are lower for local party leaders, especially when this person is also the mayor. For elected positions in municipal councils and parliament, the share of women increased from below 20 percent in the early 1970s to about 45 percent in the early 1990s, when several parties introduced gender quotas. Sweden's largest party, the Social Democrats, initiated the most important of these quotas. It raised the proportion of its women candidates elected to office at the local and national levels by about 10 percentage points by enforcing "zipped" lists with alternating female and male names on the ballot. This quota did not lead to 50 percent elected women largely because men remained overrepresented at the top rank of the ballot (for a discussion of women's political leadership and this quota policy, see O'Brien and Rickne, 2016).

Women remain more underrepresented in appointed political positions compared to elected ones. The proportion of women in local party leadership stayed well below that of the two elected positions throughout the period. It remained around 30 percent for much of the 1990s and 2000s, climbing to 40 percent only in the 2010s. The proportion of women mayors exceeded 30 percent for the first time in 2010, rose to almost 40 percent in 2014, but then dropped back down to 33 percent in 2018.

Career Gaps by Gender

We measure political careers using three binary variables. The first is re-election to the municipal council, motivated by the importance of seniority for promotion (recall Figure 1). If a person is on the ballot in the next election, the variable takes a value of 1; if they are not, it takes a value of 0. The next two variables are promotion to local party leader (all leaders and mayors, separately) and promotion to parliament. If a person moved up in the next election compared to the current election, these variables take a value of 1, and 0 otherwise. The value 0 denotes remaining in the previous position on the career ladder, moving down to a lower level, or not appearing on the ballot. The analysis sample includes municipal councilors who do not hold the position (local party leader, mayor or parliamentarian) in the current election period.

We estimate

$$Y_{imp,t+1} = \alpha + \beta Female_i + Age_{it} + \gamma_{mpt} + Sen_{it} + \epsilon_{impt} \tag{1}$$

where $Y_{imp,t+1} \in$ {re-election, leader promotion, parliament promotion in election period t+1} denotes municipal councilor i in election t, municipality m, and party p. Our coefficient of interest is β, which captures the female–male gap in the probability of re-election or promotion. Estimating Equation (1) with ordinary least squares (OLS) gives an interpretation of this coefficient in percentage points (0.01 = 1 percentage point). By including dummy variables γ_{mpt} for each combination of election, municipality, and party, we estimate this gender gap only between women and men from the same party in the same election and municipality. These dummies hold constant traits that are fixed at the election-municipality-party level, such as local party size.

We include dummy variables for politicians' birth cohort (Age_{it}) to isolate the gender comparison to women and men of the same age. We seek to compare how romantic partners matter for promotion for women and men at approximately the same stage of their lives. The age control removes career gaps related to women's younger age in earlier elections (when more women than men were political newcomers) and men's overrepresentation in older cohorts, when advancement is also less common due to retirement. Excluding the age control yields approximately 20 percent larger gender gaps (see Table 1).

To analyze promotions to local party leader and parliament, we report estimates with and without dummy variables for seniority in the regression equation (the politician's number of previous periods as a councilor, from 0 to 5+, i.e., the categorization from Figure 1). We do this to quantify the fraction of gender gaps in promotion that come from women's lower likelihood of being re-elected and to identify which gaps exist conditional on this important qualification.

The estimation results in Table 1 establish that women politicians are less likely to be promoted than men. The exception is promotions from municipal politics to parliament. On average, women are 4–5 percentage points less likely to be re-elected to the municipal council—a 9 percent difference relative to the global re-election rate of 0.58 (columns 1 and 2). They are 1 percentage point (39 percent) less likely to be promoted to local party leader, and 1 percentage point (71 percent) less likely to be promoted to mayor.

Comparing the estimates with and without fixed effects for seniority lets us comment on the relationship between the re-election and promotion results. Women's lower likelihood of re-election implies that they will accumulate less seniority than men; women are also more likely to be newcomers to politics, especially in the earliest election in our data. Holding seniority constant in columns (3) and (5) for promotions to party leader and mayor, respectively, reduces the size of the gender gaps somewhat. Yet a large proportion of the gap remains, which underscores that women are less likely to be promoted than men *and* are at a disadvantage in accumulating seniority by failing to get re-elected.

Our finding that women are not at a disadvantage for promotion to parliament is obviously good news. In fact, women have a slight advantage if we restrict the comparison to women and men who have served the same number of terms in

Table 1 Female–male promotion gaps

	DV: Re-Election = 1	DV: Promotion to Local Leader = 1		DV: Promotion to Mayor = 1		DV: Promotion to Parliament	
	(1)	(2)	(3)	(4)	(5)	(6)	(7)
Female = 1	−0.053***	−0.012***	−0.010***	−0.012***	−0.010***	0.001	0.002***
	(0.003)	(0.001)	(0.001)	(0.001)	(0.001)	(0.000)	(0.000)
Observations	169,327	65,830	65,830	43,502	43,502	169,078	169,078
DV Average	0.583	0.031	0.031	0.019	0.019	0.007	0.007
% of DV Average	−9%	−39%	−32%	−71%	−59%	14%	29%
Age FE	x	x	x	x	x	x	x
Seniority FE			x		x		x
Election-municipality-party FE	x	x	x	x	x	x	x

Notes: The table presents the results of estimating Equation (1) with OLS. The sample is municipal councilors who were not party leaders in election t from parties with representation in parliament. The analysis of re-election and promotion to parliament uses data from 1973 to 2018; the other analysis is from 1982 to 2018. The party leader promotion analysis further excludes local parties with four or fewer elected councilors, and the mayor analysis is restricted to the mayoral party in $t+1$. The outcome variables are dummies for being re-elected or promoted to local party leader, mayor, or parliamentarian in $t+1$. Seniority dummies are dummy variables for the number of previous election periods as a municipal councilor, from 0 to 5+. Age dummies are one dummy for each birth year.

municipal politics. This pattern for promotions to parliament is likely explained by the existence of party-based gender quotas and greater transparency in the nomination process, even in parties without quotas. These produce an almost identical share of women at the municipal and parliamentary levels. Women's slight advantage in these promotions is needed for the share to be equal, as women also have lower re-election rates at the local level which results in lower levels of seniority. However, women's persistent underrepresentation among local party leaders and mayors remains a concern regardless of these results, because these positions involve substantial political power and visibility.

Although we do not study appointed positions at the national level, women are underrepresented in most of these positions. The first woman prime minister was in power for about a year (2021–2022). Of the nine parties in parliament, one has never had a female party leader (the Sweden Democrats), three have had one female leader (the Conservatives, Liberals, and Christian Democrats), and two have had two female leaders (the Social Democrats and the Left Party). The Green Party is the only one with equal representation by design, since it always has two leaders of different genders.

We find no systematic variation when estimating the gender differences in re-election and promotion rates over time and across parties. All parties exhibit a negative re-election gap, women are less likely to become local leaders in all parties except the Green Party (which displays a positive but non-significant relationship), and there is a positive gender gap in promotions for parliament in all parties except the Left Party (which has a negative coefficient, very close to zero).[4] Re-running the analysis by decade reveals small (and no systematic) differences over time.

Of course, the gender-equal pattern of promotions to parliament does not rule out the possibility that women's promotions accrue higher personal costs than men's due to greater stress and strain on their relationships. We explore this prospect in Section 6.

4 Politicians' Romantic Relationships

Research on politicians' family situations has documented large gender disparities. Women politicians are less likely to be married and have children, and they have fewer children than their male counterparts (Dodson, 1997; Fulton et al., 2006; Campbell and Childs, 2014; Thomas and Bittner, 2017). A recent cross-country comparison of these family gaps among more than 4,000 parliamentarians

---

[4] We did not run the analysis by party for mayors since they are very unlikely to be from smaller parties.

in twenty-five countries showed larger gaps in low- and middle-income countries than in high-income countries (Joshi and Goehrung, 2021).

We describe two aspects of Swedish politicians' romantic relationships. The first replicates previous research by taking into account whether politicians have romantic partners and children, and if they are divorced. The second goes into depth about politicians' relationship structures to determine how the partners divide their time between paid and unpaid work. The figures in this section are descriptive; some of the differences, especially comparing politicians to the general population, relate to age differences between the groups. Since the patterns are interesting from the perspective of descriptive representation, we do not adjust for age. This helps us pinpoint the ways in which voters and political representatives may differ from each other.

Do Politicians Have Romantic Partners and Children?

Our sample includes politicians who are married or cohabiting with a partner. Cohabitation is common in Sweden; these partnerships have largely the same legal protections and responsibilities as spouses under Swedish law. Annual information on marriage, cohabitations, and divorce comes from the Swedish Marriage Register (*Äktenskapsregistret*) and the Total Population Register (*Registret över totalbefolkningen*). Cohabitations are measured with some minor measurement error before the 2014 election. Before that year, administrative data on cohabitation was available for couples who had a child together or who lived in a private dwelling (with or without child), but not for cohabitants without children living in rental apartments. A new government register for apartments was created and made available for research, which corrected this error. This is reflected in the upward shift in partnerships in 2014 in Figure 3. Same-sex couples were able to register their relationship starting in 1995 and marry in 2009; they make up 0.1 percent of all couples in our data. Even in the last elections when same-sex marriages were allowed, they make up fewer than 0.5 percent of the couples in our sample.

Figure 3 displays the proportions of partnered politicians (top) and divorced politicians (bottom) over time by politician sex and career level. The green lines denote rates in the Swedish population aged eighteen and above. The figure establishes that women politicians at all career levels are somewhat less likely to have partners than their male counterparts. Averaging all available election years, women politicians are about 8 percentage points (10 percent) less likely to have a romantic partner; this gap is larger at higher career levels and smaller at lower ones. The gap has also declined over time. Women parliamentarians were 23.5 percentage points less likely to be partnered in the 1970s, 15.7

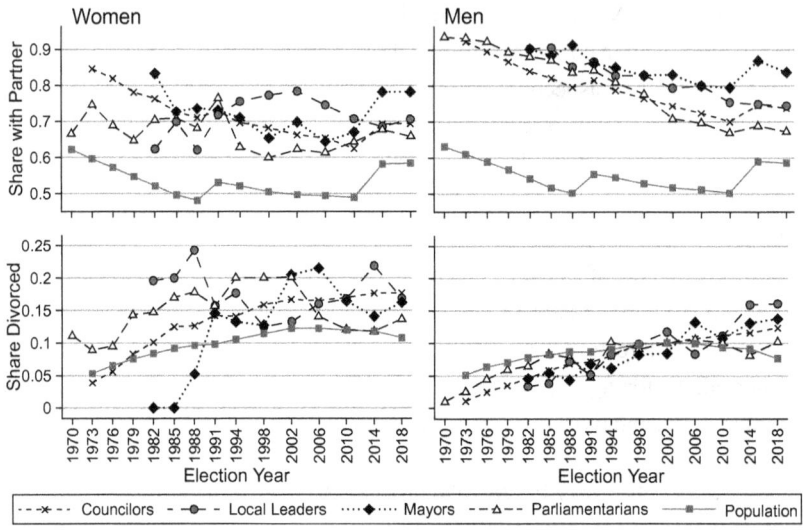

Figure 3 Proportions of partnered and divorced politicians.

Notes: The figure depicts the proportions of politicians who have a romantic partner (top) and are divorced (bottom) by sex at birth, career level, and election.

percentage points less likely in the 1990s and 1 percentage point less likely in the 2010s. The figure also shows that politicians of both sexes are more likely than the average Swedish adult to have a partner. This gap relative to the adult population is larger for men than for women, especially in the earliest election periods in our data. In the later periods it remains high for mayors relative to parliamentarians, likely due to party composition. Mayorships are more often held by Social Democrats or Conservatives, while parliamentarians have more recently come to consist more of Sweden Democrats—a radical right party that has grown dramatically since entering parliament in 2010. This party has a large proportion of male politicians, especially men who are single or divorced (Dal Bó et al., 2023). While the finding that politicians are more likely to have a partner is partly a consequence of the politicians' age distribution, it is interesting from the perspective of descriptive representation since nonpartnered voters have far fewer representatives in political office.

Women politicians are substantially more likely to be divorced than men. This pattern reflects a broader phenomenon in the adult Swedish population in which men who divorce are more likely to remarry and do so faster than women who divorce. However, the divorce gap is only 1.8 percentage points in the population, while it is 6.3 percentage points among politicians. The larger gender gap among politicians comes entirely from a higher divorce rate among women in politics, which aligns with the expectations of our career stress hypothesis. The gap

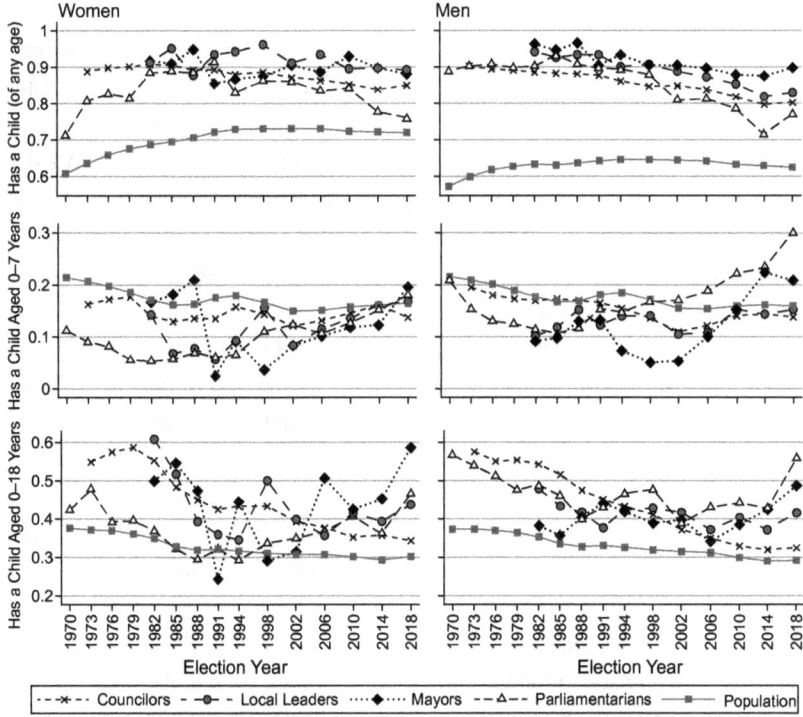

Figure 4 Proportions of politicians who are parents.

Notes: Information on the birth year of all children come from administrative records.

reflects greater stress and tension in women's relationships when women progress up the political career ladder if they shoulder a larger household burden and their husband expects his career to be prioritized.

Figure 4 depicts the overall share of politicians who are parents and the share that have children in different age categories. It establishes that a large proportion of politicians are parents and reveals no apparent gender gaps. Politicians of both genders are substantially more likely to be parents compared to the general population, and women politicians are not less likely to have children or to have young children. Women parliamentarians in the 1970 election (the first election for which we can observe parliamentarians) are a notable exception to this pattern: 70 percent of the women and 90 percent of the men were parents, but this gap had disappeared by the early 1980s.

Levels of Career Support in Politicians' Relationships

In this section we examine how women and men politicians split paid and unpaid work with their romantic partners. Revisiting the intuition from our theory section, these time divisions constitute measurements of career support provided by the politician's partner. When the politician earns a larger share of the household earnings, it indicates that the couple prioritizes the politician's career by having them invest more time in paid work relative to their partner. Conversely, when the politician does a smaller share of the household's care work, it indicates that their partner supports their career by taking on a larger share of the domestic workload.

We use tax record data to calculate the division of paid work. We measure the time and energy dedicated to paid work as each partner's earnings from all jobs and business ownership in each calendar year. This lets us calculate the politician's share of the couple's total earnings. For politicians in unpaid positions, we can calculate this variable contemporaneously in the election year. For those holding the paid positions of mayor and parliamentarian, we go backward in the tax record data to the first year before they obtained that position and use the earnings division from that year. This avoids measurement error in the intrahousehold earnings distribution as a measurement of support in the political career. Once a politician obtains a full-time position, their wage is in the top 5 percent of the Swedish earnings distribution. If either spouse is over sixty years old, we go back to the year when both spouses were under sixty to avoid measurement error from retirement income replacing earned income.

Using the division of earnings to evaluate the level of career support could introduce a measurement error because low earnings in the labor market do not necessarily signify a high share of care and household work. It could also indicate a long-term illness or another time-demanding unpaid activity, such as being a student or partaking in an active labor market program. We (imperfectly) adjust for this potential error by removing couples if the politician earns 100 percent of the household income (5 percent of all municipal councilors). Using Statistics Sweden's categorization of people's main economic activity in the calendar year, which is based on various administrative records, politicians who make 100 percent of household earnings have partners who are on disability pension (23 percent), old-age pension (16 percent), economic support as a full-time caretaker for a child or relative (9 percent), active labor market program (8 percent), sickness benefits (6 percent), or a student (6 percent). Only 23 percent are classified as having "no income," which means they have no income from other government programs that would classify them as another category, a group that would include "legitimate" stay-at-home partners. Most people in the "no income" group do not have children under eighteen; thus stay-at-home parents comprise only a small fraction of this group. We do not remove the handful of couples in which the politician makes 0 percent of household earnings since they are too few to affect the analysis. While this adjustment is correct on average, it likely excludes some legitimate stay-at-home partners from the analysis.

We calculate the division of unpaid work using data from the Swedish Social Insurance Agency for (1) parental leave and (2) temporary parental leave. Parental leave data come from the longitudinal integration database for health insurance and labor market studies (LISA, according to its Swedish acronym) after 1990 and from the Income and Taxation Register (*Inkomst- och taxeringsregistret*) before this year. Temporary parental leave data is from the Income and Taxation Register. Both capture unpaid care work in the household, which allows us to calculate the partner's share; a higher level indicates that the politician enjoys a higher level of career support. Since the data on both parental leave and temporary parental leave are only available starting in 1981, we do not have these measures for politicians elected to municipal councils or parliament in the 1970s.

The Swedish parental leave system is administered entirely by the government. Leave periods are processed centrally, which creates a detailed administrative record. We compute the division of parental leave based on data for parental leave payments, which is available for the full period, and cross-check this variable against data on the number of days of leave, which is only available from 1993. We sum up the leave for the first three years of life for all children that a couple has, including adopted children. Parental leave is a meaningful measurement of the division of unpaid work in Sweden for two reasons. First, parental leave is long: 90 percent of couples take at least twelve months of full-time leave per child. Second, how this leave is shared between the parents is strongly correlated with the division of other unpaid domestic work in the household (Kotsadam and Finseraas, 2011).[5]

Parental leave may be a short-term shock, yet it has been shown to have long-term consequences. The gender wage gap commonly starts at the arrival of the first child (Kleven et al., 2019), especially in high-earning groups. In line with expectations from Goldin's (2014) theory, Azmat et al (2022) demonstrate that women are substantially less likely to have high-status jobs that require their presence in the workplace after having children. An important reason for this gendered development in the labor market can be attributed to women using substantially larger shares of the very generous parental leave in Sweden (Angelov et al., 2016).

---

[5] Before 1974, paid parental leave was 180 days for mothers, which changed that year to six months of leave that could be used by either parent. The leave gradually lengthened to 480 days, three months of which is earmarked for each parent. Parents' right to parental leave is protected by law, and firms cannot deny it during the first eighteen months of the child's life; they can only deny unpaid leave after that age. Childcare generally does not admit children under one year of age.

Temporary (paid) parental leave is available to parents who stay home from work to take care of a sick child aged eight months to eleven years. An employee can take up to 120 days of leave per year and receive 80 percent of their wages (capped at the equivalent of roughly US$ 30,000 per year). An individual must report the leave to the Social Insurance Agency to receive compensation, which (again) generates administrative records tied to their personal identification code. The system is widely used: about two-thirds of couples with children under eleven use it at some point in each calendar year, and the average parent uses 3.7 days per year (authors' calculations). We calculate the romantic partner's share of days, pooling days for all years in which the couple had children under ten years old. Using temporary parental leave to measure household work is well established in the literature. Eriksson and Nermo (2010) detected a strong relationship between temporary parental leave and hours spent in the household. Ichino et al. (2023) confirm that fathers' take-up of temporary parental leave is strongly correlated with their self-reported time spent on domestic chores like cleaning, cooking, and repair work.

Our three measurements of spousal support—earnings share, parental leave, and temporary parental leave—are interconnected theoretically as well as empirically in three ways. First, the relationship between earnings share and temporary parental leave has been established leveraging tax reforms to study shifts in the disposable income of the man or the woman in a couple. The change in earnings share affects the home production shares (measured in days of temporary parental leave), in line with the expectations of specialization theory (Eriksson and Nermo, 2010; Ichino et al., 2023). Second, there is a strong correlation between fathers' parental leave and their share of temporary parental leave (Ekberg et al., 2013). Third, women's absence from the labor market after they have children is a driving source of gender differences in pay and time investment in the labor market (Kleven et al., 2019; Azmat et al., 2022). Importantly, spousal support in terms of parental leave is more than just a way for women to acquire more time in the labor market. Spousal parental leave is particularly beneficial for mothers' earnings. Each month of parental leave a father takes has a more substantial positive impact on maternal earnings than an equivalent reduction in the mother's own leave (Johansson, 2010).

Figure 5 plots time use patterns in male and female politicians' romantic partnerships. Higher values of all three variables indicate a higher level of career support for the politician from their romantic partner. Male politicians (right column) have higher levels of support on all three measurements.

The average woman politician makes a lower share of household income than the average male politician at each career level. Among councilors and local

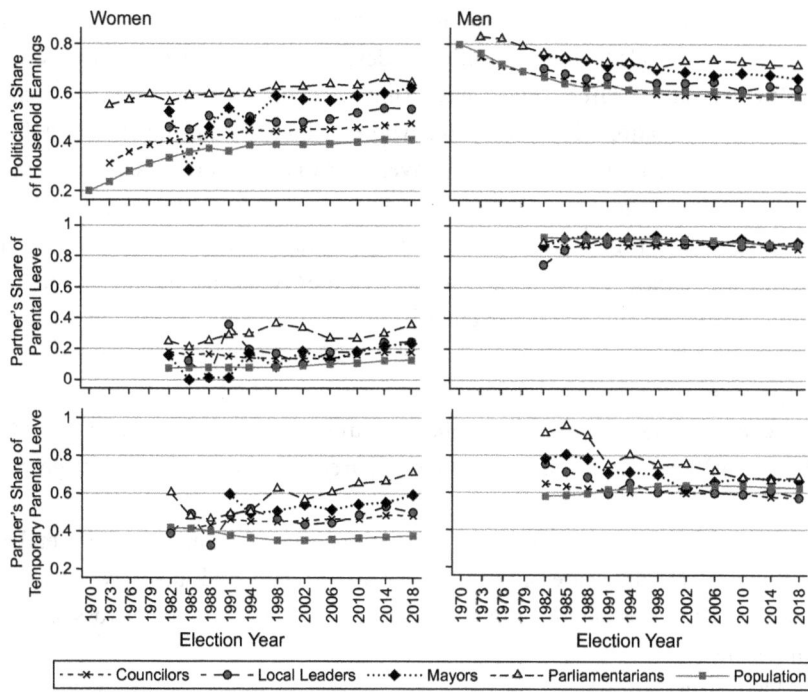

Figure 5 Division of paid and unpaid work in politicians' romantic relationships.

Notes: The figure plots descriptive statistics for three measurements of the time division in Swedish households (green lines) and among politicians (gray or black lines). Annual earnings include all income sources from wages or business income. Parental leave is measured using payment data from the Social Insurance Agency, and temporary parental leave is measured in days. These two measures sum up all leave for eligible children in the household per year.

party leaders, the average woman earns 45 percent of household earnings and the average male politician earns 62 percent. For mayors and parliamentarians, the average woman earns about 60 percent and the average man a little over 70 percent. It is notable for this variable that politicians in higher office make a larger percentage of household earnings than lower-level politicians, which suggests that having a relationship that prioritizes the politician's career is conducive to promotion.

Looking at the division of unpaid work, women again enjoy less career support than men. The average romantic partner of women politicians has taken just 16 percent of the couple's total parental leave, while the average partner of male politicians has taken 87 percent. The corresponding figures for temporary parental leave are 45 percent and 61 percent.

Comparing politicians' divisions of labor to those in the Swedish adult population reveals that male politicians deviate much less than women. Male politicians at all career levels have similar labor divisions as men in the Swedish population. By contrast, the women who enter and advance in politics have partners who provide above average career support. It is also striking from the figure how women's departure from the population grows across career levels. At the lower level of municipal councilor, the average woman politician already has a somewhat more supportive romantic partner on all three variables, but this difference becomes very large at the top levels. Women mayors and parliamentarians earn a 20-percentage-point (50 percent) larger share of household earnings than the average adult woman, and they have taken about half of the household's parental leave (10 percentage points less) and 30 percent less of the temporary parental leave (15 percentage points less).

As in Section 3, we find no major or systematic party differences. The gender differences for the share of politicians who are partnered, divorced, or have children, as well as the shares of paid and unpaid work, are similar across parties (not shown).

The results in this section replicates some descriptive results for "family gaps" between women and men politicians in previous research but also provides new insights. Women are somewhat less likely to have a romantic partner, which we show is partly because they are more likely to be divorced. Yet contrary to previous research, we do not find that women are less likely to have children, which may be attributable to Sweden's generous systems of childcare and parental leave. Our detailed data on time divisions within households reveal that male politicians enjoy more career support from their romantic partners than female politicians. This is reflected in their larger shares of paid work and smaller shares of unpaid work relative to their partners. These time divisions likely enable men to advance in their political careers. Women politicians have less career support than male politicians, but more than the average adult woman in the population; the gender gap in support narrows at higher political levels. For women to advance in politics, they need a partner who is willing to depart from the norm, which may lead to stress and tension as women advance in their political careers.

5 Romantic Partners as a Source of Career Inequality

Our theoretical framework connects differences across women's and men's romantic partnerships to the gender gap in political careers. We derive a *Career support hypothesis*, which predicts that *women's lower level of career support from their romantic partners can help explain their slower career advancement in politics*. We now test this prediction and its auxiliary hypothesis—that spousal support matters more when politicians have children.

The analysis in this section builds directly on the previous two. Section 3 documented a disadvantage for women in promotions to appointed political positions in local government. Women were less likely to accumulate seniority by getting re-elected, and less likely to be promoted to local party leader or mayor conditional on their seniority level. Section 4 brought another piece of the puzzle by showing that women's romantic relationships provide less career support than men's relationships. Women politicians are more often in relationships in which they perform a large portion of the childcare work themselves, and their career is less prioritized within the household compared to male politicians' relationships. This section combines these two analyses to test if differences in career support from romantic partners (for the roughly 90 percent of politicians in our sample who have a partner) help explain the career gap.[6]

Our empirical strategy returns to the career regressions from Section 3 (Equation 1) and adds the career support measurements from Section 4 to the regression equation. By examining how the coefficient on the binary indicator for female sex at birth changes when we add these controls, we can assess whether the gender gap in the likelihood of promotion derives from the difference in romantic partner support. In other words, we test our expectation that the gender gap in political career progression would substantially shrink if women had the same partner support as men. We use this method to determine how much of the gender gap in career progression can be explained by our measurements of paid and unpaid work. If introducing our partner support variables does not reduce the coefficients, we can conclude that differences in partner support cannot explain the gender gaps we observe in Section 3.

We conduct the analysis sequentially to account for two features of the data. The first is that our three variables for partner support are available for slightly different time periods. Second, since the division of parental leave has a very high pairwise correlation with sex at birth, we cannot generate meaningful separate estimates for the gender gap in promotion and the division of parental leave.[7]

We start by running the career regressions from Section 3, including the division of paid work (results in the top part of Table 2). Next we run

---

[6] Estimating the re-election and promotion gaps for partnered politicians only gives very similar-sized estimates as those for the full sample.

[7] The pairwise correlation is 0.86 – far above the 0.7 which is the general rule of thumb when multicollinearity precludes estimating the coefficients in a meaningful way.

Table 2 Career advancement and romantic partner support

	DV: Re-election = 1		DV: Promotion to Local Party Leader = 1		DV: Promotion to Mayor = 1	
	(1)	(2)	(3)	(4)	(5)	(6)
Female = 1	−0.047***	−0.031***	−0.012***	−0.008***	−0.010***	−0.006***
	(0.003)	(0.004)	(0.002)	(0.002)	(0.002)	(0.002)
Politician's Share of Household Earnings		0.082***		0.025***		0.019***
		(0.009)		(0.005)		(0.004)
Earnings' Share = 1		−0.058***		−0.016***		−0.014***
		(0.007)		(0.004)		(0.004)
Observations	115,542	115,542	44,167	44,167	29,915	29,915
DV Average	0.590		0.028		0.015	
Coefficient Reduction in Percent		−34%		−33%		−40%
Female = 1	−0.041***	−0.011	−0.015***	−0.009**	−0.015***	−0.007*
	(0.007)	(0.007)	(0.003)	(0.003)	(0.003)	(0.004)
Politician's Share of Household Earnings		0.154***		0.025***		0.018*
		(0.018)		(0.009)		(0.010)
Earnings' Share = 1		−0.113***		−0.022**		−0.017*
		(0.019)		(0.009)		(0.009)
Partner's Share of Temporary Parental Leave		0.033***		0.013**		0.028***
		(0.012)		(0.006)		(0.006)

Observations	30,625	30,625	17,991	17,991	10,686	10,686
DV Average		0.632		0.058		0.060
Coefficient Reduction in Percent		−70%		−40%		−53%
Age fixed effects		x		x		x
Election-municipality-party FE		x		x		x

Notes: The table shows regression estimates from estimating Equation (1) with and without variables for the politician's share of household earnings (top) and share of household earnings and temporary parental leave (bottom). The sample is municipal councilors who are not ranked first on their party's ballot and who were elected in a municipality where their party holds five or more seats in the municipal assembly. For local party leaders, political parties are included if they hold at least one seat in parliament. The analysis for mayors includes the largest parties in the governing majority. Standard errors in parentheses, *** $p < 0.01$, ** $p < 0.05$, * $p < 0.1$.

regressions with the division of paid work and temporary parental leave, our first proxy for the division of unpaid work (bottom part of Table 2). For the earnings division, we include both the continuous variable (0–1) and two dummies for the end points of this scale, politicians making either 100 percent or 0 percent of household earnings. This helps address the measurement error discussed in Section 2, where divisions of earnings at the end points of this scale often reflect sick or disabled partners. We report the gender gap in re-election in the first two columns and then estimate the gaps in leadership appointments to local party leaders and mayors. We run these regressions without holding seniority constant. While our previous observation that women are less likely to receive leadership promotions for the same level of seniority was relevant to characterize the nature of the gender career gaps, seniority is an endogenous variable here because romantic partners help determine re-election, which in turn helps determine promotions. This makes seniority a "bad control" in our promotion regressions by netting out an important mechanism.

The sign and size of the coefficients on career support variables in Table 2 support our general assumptions about how support from romantic partners helps politicians advance. If a politician's career is prioritized within the household (i.e., when the politician makes a larger share of total household earnings), they are more likely to be re-elected and promoted. The coefficient on the dummy for earning 100 percent of the household's income is negative, which likely reflects the negative career impact of needing to provide care for the romantic partner in a sizable fraction of these households. The coefficient on the partner's share of temporary leave also takes the expected positive sign: a larger share of leave taken by the politician's partner is associated with a higher probability of being re-elected and promoted.

Our main results come from inspecting how the size of the gender gaps in re-election and promotion probabilities change when we control for partner support. This amounts to comparing the estimate on the dummy for female sex at birth from the regressions without the career support variables (odd-numbered columns of Table 2) to those after adding these controls (even-numbered columns). We simplify the assessment of the results by reporting the change in the size of the coefficient between each pair of regressions relative to the averages of the dependent variable in the bottom row of each panel.

Holding constant the division of paid work in politicians' households explains about one-third of women politicians' lower likelihood of advancing in their career. The re-election gap shrinks by 34 percent (from 4.7 to 3.1 percentage points); the promotion gap to local party leader decreases by 33 percent and to mayor by 40 percent. Next, we include the division of paid *and* unpaid work for the smaller time period for which both are available (1982–2018). This sample is considerably smaller because politicians need to have had at least one child after 1982 to have an observable division of temporary parental leave. Women's re-election gap is slightly smaller in this subsample, while the promotion gap is larger. Adding the two controls accounts for 40–70 percent of the promotion gaps, 70 percent for re-election, 40 percent for promotion to local party leader, and 53 percent for promotion to mayor.

We cannot add the division of parental leave to the analysis in Table 2 due to the strong statistical relationship between the sex of the politician and the partner's parental leave. Ideally, we would like to compare men and women with partners who have taken similar shares of parental leave. However, there is very little overlap in men's and women's distribution. For example, while 93 percent of men have a partner who has taken more than 50 percent of the parental leave, only 4 percent of women do. We sidestep this issue by comparing women and men depending on whether they had a relatively gender-equal split of their parental leave or a relatively traditional split. We subdivide the sample based on the median for the *female partner's* share of the leave, which is 95 percent in the data. This lets us compare the promotion probabilities for women and men in relationships in which the split was relatively unequal to those with a relatively equal split, subsamples that now include meaningful fractions of both female and male politicians.

The results in Table 3 show smaller gender gaps in career advancement for politicians who split parental leave more gender equally (even-numbered columns) relative to less gender equally (odd-numbered columns). The gap in re-election drops by 16 percent in progressive couples (not significant) while the gap in party leader promotion drops by 43 percent and for promotion to mayor by 65 percent.

As in Sections 3 and 4, we find no major or systematic differences across parties or over time (not shown). The gender differences in re-election and promotion rates are generally reduced after we introduce our measurements of paid and unpaid work; for those that reach statistical significance, the coefficients are in the expected direction.[8]

The results in this section suggest that career support from a romantic partner helps politicians advance professionally. Lower levels of career support for women compared to men account for about half of women's lower probability of getting re-elected and appointed to leadership appointments in subnational Swedish politics.

---

[8] As there are no systematic differences across parties and over time so far, and the subsample analysis has limited statistical power, we do not proceed with analyses by party and over time in the remaining analyses, which employ a smaller sample size.

Table 3 Career advancement by parental leave-division in politicians' household

Female Partner's Share of Parental Leave:	DV: Re-election = 1		DV: Promotion to Local Party Leader = 1		DV: Promotion to Mayor = 1	
	Below Median (1)	Above Median (2)	Below Median (3)	Above Median (4)	Below Median (5)	Above Median (6)
Female = 1	−0.050***	−0.042***	−0.021***	−0.012**	−0.026***	−0.009*
	(0.008)	(0.008)	(0.005)	(0.005)	(0.005)	(0.005)
Observations	30,625	30,625	17,991	17,991	10,686	10,686
DV Average	0.585	0.605	0.047	0.043	0.033	0.031
Coefficient Reduction in Percent	−16%		−43%		−65%	
Age Fixed Effects	x	x	x	x	x	x
Election-muni-party FE	x	x	x	x	x	x

Notes: The table shows estimates for regression Equation (1) in subsamples based on the median for the wife's share of parental leave.

Partner Career Support around First Parenthood

Our career support hypothesis predicts that career support from a romantic partner is particularly important in explaining women politicians' career disadvantage after they have children. An important factor in analyzing this question is the fraction of politicians who have children *after* starting their political career. Our description of politicians' family situations above showed that 90 percent of elected municipal councilors and parliamentarians of both genders are parents. Figure 6 graphs the length of time between politicians' first year as a municipal councilor and the birth year of their first child. It indicates that 90 percent were already parents when they started their political career. This is also true for subsample of politicians who eventually became local party leaders. Among men who later became mayors, slightly more (16 percent) entered politics before having their first child, but this does not explain the gender gap in promotions to mayor. Interestingly, even though a lower share of female mayors became politicians before having their first child, they still entered politics at a younger age than male mayors (thirty-seven years vs. thirty-nine years for men).

A key reason that people have children before entering politics is that most political careers start at a later age, when most people have already had their first child. Thus low career support from the romantic partner after the birth of the first child cannot be an important factor in women's career disadvantage. Too few politicians in our sample have their first child after entering politics. This insight also has policy relevance for work conditions that might help combat career inequalities. Politicians' access to parental leave or other work conditions related to early parenthood, such as the availability of lactation rooms, should of course not be ignored but are likely less important in politics than in other sectors of the labor market. Political jobs (including full-time jobs such as mayors) do not count as jobs in Sweden and therefore do not qualify for parental leave benefits beyond the basic coverage that a non-working person would receive. While these rules are designed to avoid professionalizing political appointments, some municipalities offer special parental leave schemes to avoid disincentivizing parenthood or discouraging people who wish to be parents from seeking these positions.[9]

If parenthood shifts couples' division of labor in a gender-traditional direction, we should observe that women experience a larger career disadvantage when they give birth or when their children are small. If our auxiliary prediction is correct, our variables for romantic partner support should be more important for explaining these larger post-parenthood gaps than the smaller gaps pre-parenthood.

---

[9] For a discussion of work conditions and gender inequality in politics, see Palmieri (2018).

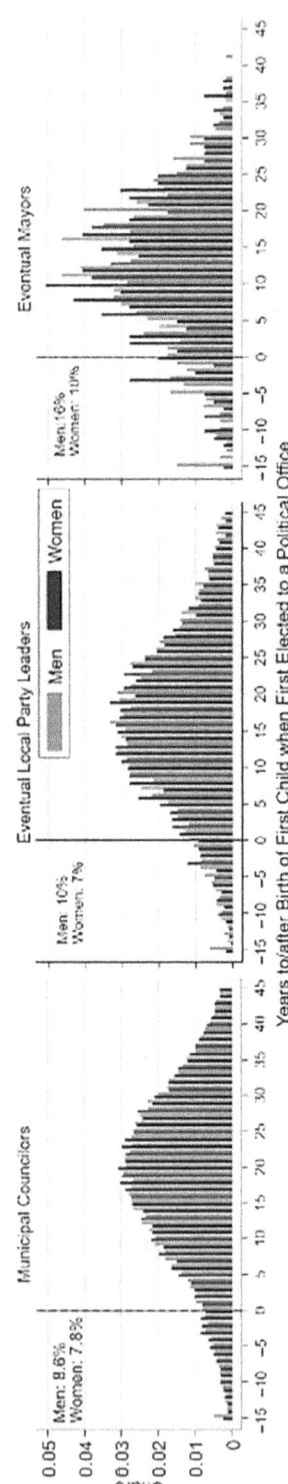

Figure 6 Time durations between entry into politics and parenthood.

Notes: The figure plots the distribution of the time between politicians' entry into politics as a municipal councilor and the birth of their first child (in one-year bins). The middle and right graphs restrict the sample to politicians who later became local party leaders and mayors.

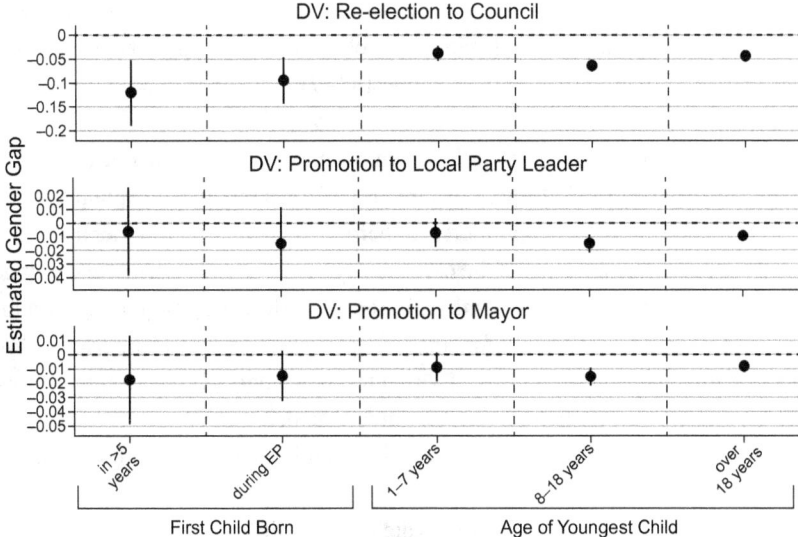

Figure 7 Female–male career gaps by parenthood and child ages.

Notes: The figure displays estimates from Equation (1) for different subsamples of municipal councilors, denoted on the x-axis. The sample split on the left compares estimates for councilors who became parents more than five years later to those who had a child between t and $t+1$ (during Election Period). The split on the left separates parents based on the age of their youngest child in election year t. The vertical lines denote 95 percent confidence intervals.

Comparing career gaps based on parenthood status and children's ages does not reveal evidence of expanding gaps post-parenthood. We compare the gender gaps in re-election and promotion in election $t+1$ between municipal councilors who were at least five years before parenthood in election t, and those who became a parent between elections t and $t+1$ (Figure 7). There is no consistent pattern of growing gaps post-parenthood. If anything, the gap in re-election declines and the gap in promotion to party leader increases slightly, but there is no difference in promotion to the most important leadership position (mayor). One reason for the lack of a difference might be that the politics sector experiences a higher turnover of young people than the private labor market, and that women are more likely to leave politics in those age groups. For employed (paid) politicians, the arrival of children might motivate them to change to a more flexible type of job. For unpaid politicians, having children might cause them to prioritize their nonpolitical career and step down from their political appointment.[10]

---

[10] People who enter local politics in high school often quit when they move to a university town, and most people who participate in local politics during university or college quit when they

The right-hand side of Figure 7 runs a similar comparison based on the age of the politician's youngest child. We do not observe larger gaps between women and men whose children are the youngest (1–7) compared to politicians with older children.

Even if political career gaps between women and men do not obviously widen after parenthood, the partner support variables might still explain a larger fraction of the gap after parenthood than before. To determine whether this is the case, we repeat the analysis of the explanatory power of the division of earnings in the subsample of parents with children of different ages (the small subsamples preclude a meaningful analysis of temporary parental leave). We present this analysis in Table 4. Two factors are important when interpreting these results: how much the estimated career gap decreases after controlling for the politician's share of household earnings, and the estimated importance of this factor for promotion.

The results reported in Table 4 indicate no clear differences in the importance of the division of household earnings between politicians with younger or older children. For each three outcomes and each three subsamples, the estimated gender gap is reduced substantially and has a similar absolute magnitude when we introduce a control for the politician's share of household earnings. In relative terms this reduction is the largest among politicians with small children, but this is because the initial gap is the smallest in this subsample. The estimated coefficient on the division of household earnings is also similar, which points to the general importance of romantic partner support irrespective of the time constraints imposed by the presence of small children in the household.

6 Political Promotions and Relationship Stress

Just as a romantic partner can be a crucial source of career support, they can also be a source of negative stress and tension for an ambitious politician. As we laid out in Section 2, political positions are often demanding in terms of time and personal engagement. Advancing to higher positions involves high learning costs and significant time investments. Top positions in local and national politics often involve long and unpredictable work hours, as well as long commutes in the case of national politics.[11]

The TV show *Borgen* depicts the damage an unsupportive romantic partner can do to a politician's quality of life. When female protagonist Birgitte Nyborg becomes the Danish prime minister, her husband complains about her absence

---

graduate and leave that municipality. Swedish women have been more likely than men to attend and graduate from tertiary education since the 1970s.

[11] The analysis in this section relies heavily on previously published results in Folke and Rickne (2020).

Table 4 Career advancement and romantic partner support, depending on children's ages

	DV: Re-election = 1		DV: Promotion to Local Party Leader = 1		DV: Promotion to Mayor = 1	
	(1)	(2)	(3)	(4)	(5)	(6)
Sample: At least one small child (0–7 years) in election year t						
Female = 1	−0.025***	−0.009	−0.006	−0.000	−0.001	0.008
	(0.008)	(0.010)	(0.005)	(0.006)	(0.005)	(0.006)
Politician's Share of Household Earnings		0.062***		0.026*		0.040***
		(0.020)		(0.014)		(0.013)
Observations	20,216	20,216	6,656	6,656	4,348	4,348
Sample: At least one young child (8–18 years), no small children in election year t						
Female = 1	−0.056***	−0.038***	−0.015***	−0.011***	−0.013***	−0.011***
	(0.006)	(0.006)	(0.004)	(0.004)	(0.003)	(0.004)
Politician's Share of Household Earnings		0.082***		0.018*		0.013
		(0.015)		(0.010)		(0.009)
Observations	40,905	40,905	13,185	13,185	9,375	9,375
Sample: Only adult children (over 18 years) in election year t						
Female = 1	−0.049***	−0.034***	−0.012***	−0.007***	−0.009***	−0.005**
	(0.005)	(0.005)	(0.002)	(0.002)	(0.002)	(0.002)

Table 4 (cont.)

	DV: Re-election = 1		DV: Promotion to Local Party Leader = 1		DV: Promotion to Mayor = 1	
	(1)	(2)	(3)	(4)	(5)	(6)
Politician's Share of Household Earnings		0.089*** (0.013)		0.030*** (0.005)		0.025*** (0.005)
Observations	53,012	53,012	21,949	21,949	14,773	14,773
Only Earner Dummy		x		x		x
Age Fixed Effects	x	x	x	x	x	x
Election-muni-party FE	x	x	x	x	x	x

Notes: The table presents estimates from regression Equation (1) with added controls for the politician's share of household earnings in even-numbered columns. The sample is municipal councilors who are parents; the sample is split based on the age of their youngest child in election year t.

from home even though he initially claimed to fully support her ambitions. Birgitte is miserable when the relationship breaks down as her husband is unable to handle her elevated social status and demanding work schedule. The fictional character has parallels in real life. Finland's first female prime minister Sanna Marin divorced in 2023 after four years in power, and French National Front leader Marine Le Pen has been divorced twice. U.S. political firebrands Marjorie Taylor Green and Lauren Boebert are both divorced.

Theoretical frameworks suggest that couple formation patterns may underpin a gender inequality in the personal price than male and female politicians pay to be promoted (recall the discussion in Section 2). Social norms lead many women to "marry up" and men to "marry down" in terms of their partner's age and economic earning power in the labor market. These relationship patterns prevail even among women who graduate from top educational programs (Ely et al. 2014). They imply that most relationships prioritize the male partner's career when deciding how to organize their joint time use and effort. A husband's eventual promotion to a top job aligns with this prioritization, while the wife's promotion contradicts it, a fact that may lead to stress and tension as the couple needs to renegotiate their relationship (Becker et al., 1977; Coverman, 1989).

We study stress and tension in politicians' relationships by analyzing how political promotions affect the likelihood that they will divorce. Divorce is the culmination of previous stress in the relationship, and causes additional mental and economic hardship. It therefore represents a high personal cost of political advancement. Even if leaving a bad relationship is often better than staying, the best outcome would have been to remain in a stable, supportive union. Based on current relationship patterns, such stable supportive unions are more likely for men who get promoted than for women. People generally strive for such unions; 98 percent of Swedish male and female respondents to the World Values Survey (WVS) reported that "Family" is "important" or "very important" in their lives (authors' calculations using 2010 WVS data).

Section 3 revealed higher divorce rates among women than men in all political positions. It also established that there are elevated divorce rates among women in politics relative to women in the general Swedish population; male politicians do not exhibit this pattern. These data suggest that political positions may put pressure on women's relationships that their male colleagues do not face.

Empirical Methodology

We compare whether a politician's marriage ends in divorce depending on whether they were promoted to mayor or parliamentarian or not. This analysis can identify a causal effect of promotion on divorce by comparing the relationships of close contenders for these two promotions.

We define close contenders for *parliament* as candidates who are near the electoral margin on parties' rank-ordered ballot papers (based on counting seats from the top of the list). For each ballot in Sweden's twenty-nine electoral districts, we define the two contenders as the last elected person (i.e., the lowest-ranked elected candidate) and the first unelected person (i.e., the highest-ranked unelected person).[12] This gives us a marginal winner and a marginal loser on each ballot.

We define close contenders for *mayor* as the local party leaders from the largest political parties in the ideological left and right blocs in each municipality. A ruling coalition typically forms within one of these blocs, making these two people rivals for the top executive post. The party leader whose bloc forms the governing majority usually becomes mayor, while the leader of the losing bloc becomes the opposition leader—a position with substantially less influence, work hours, and responsibilities (for an in-depth description of these positions, see Nilsson, 2001; Jonsson, 2003).

Parties' electoral fortunes can shift over time; individuals can be promoted, then lose that position, and regain it in the future. To account for this possibility, the promotion variable only includes individuals who have never held either of these political jobs. We allow losers to appear in the dataset more than once, but cluster standard errors at the individual level. A potential concern associated with including repeat losers is that people with more stable relationships might be overrepresented in the sample. This would happen if a person who lost an election is more likely to reappear in the sample if they did not divorce after their first loss. But bias from this sample selection is likely small, since nearly all repeated losers run again in the election immediately following their first loss. The treatment effect is *larger* if we remove the repeated losers, but the precision is reduced (results not shown in the interest of space).

We pool the two sets of contenders in six elections between 1991 and 2010 with the exception of the 1994 national election.[13] We then go back in time four years before the election in which a particular person was a contender ($t = -4$). In this year, we drop politicians who were not married, leaving 68 percent of the

---

[12] We exclude the extremely small proportion of electoral ballots (1 percent) from which preference votes determined who was elected.

[13] This election has an erroneous recording of the list rank variable. We cannot include national elections prior to 1991 because low data quality for the list rank variable precludes a precise calculations of close contenders, and we drop mayoral promotions in this time period to have balance over time in the two promotions.

men and 58 percent of the women (robustness checks indicate that the results are insensitive to changing this starting year).

We cannot study cohabitations because our data does not accurately measure dissolution of these unions. We instead use a variable for whether a person remains married because it can correctly capture divorce, conditional on removing politicians from the analysis if their spouse died near an election. Divorces are processed relatively quickly in Sweden, partly because divorce law is unilateral.[14]

The final sample includes 683 individual-election observations for women and 1,556 for men. We follow the relationship statuses of these politicians over time, starting four years prior to the election ($t = -4$), up to the election in $t = 0$, and eight years afterwards ($t = 8$). Because two married women (or men) rarely appear as contenders for the same position in the same year, we pool the two samples (as in, e.g., Eggers and Hainmueller, 2009; Kotakorpi et al., 2017).

We evaluate how the likelihood of remaining married changes over time for women and men separately. After this, we conduct a heterogeneity analysis to uncover whether divorce patterns after a promotion are related to the romantic partner's level of career support.

To estimate the treatment effect of promotion on divorce, we estimate the following regression to capture the difference between the treatment and control groups in the probability of remaining married in each year relative to the year immediately before the promotion ($t = 0$):

$$Y_{iet} = \beta_t P_{ie} * T_t + T_t + \delta_{ie} + S_{ie} * T_t + \tau_e * T_t + \varepsilon_{iet} \qquad (2)$$

In this equation, the dependent variable is a binary indicator for remaining married for politician i in election e and event year t. The vector (T_t) is a set of dummy variables for each year before or after an election, starting four years before the election ($t = -4$) and ending eight years afterwards ($t = 8$). The variable $P_{i,e}$ takes a value of 1 for promoted politicians, and 0 otherwise. We set the reference year by excluding the time dummy for the year of the election ($t = 0$). The estimates on the interactions between each time dummy and the promotion dummy (β_t) thus capture the gap in remaining married between promoted and nonpromoted people in each event year relative to the size of that gap in $t = 0$.

---

[14] In Sweden's no-fault divorce system, one spouse can receive a divorce without showing any wrongdoing by the other spouse, and couples are not required to undergo mediation or a period of living separately before the procedure is finalized. In most cases, divorce papers are processed within one month. After this, divorce law specifies a six-month cooling-off period between filing for and finalizing a divorce if at least one spouse demands such a period, or if the couple has children under sixteen.

The regression specification includes independent terms for the time dummies before and after the election (T_t), as well as interactions between these time dummies and (i) fixed effects for each election τ_e and (ii) a binary indicator for belonging to the parliamentary sample, $S_{i,e}$. These variables control for the fact that the probability of being promoted, or temporal trends in the probability of being promoted, could differ between elections and between the parliamentary and mayoral samples. We also include fixed effects for each combination of election and individual, $\delta_{i,e}$ (recall that losing candidates can appear multiple times), and cluster standard errors at the level of the individual politician. Note that the structure of Equation (2) makes it redundant to control for the independent terms of $S_{i,e}$, τ_t, and $P_{i,e}$.

Descriptive Results

Figure 8 illustrates trends in remaining married for women and men politicians who are either promoted to parliament or mayor or not. Trend lines start at 1 in event year $t = -4$ since we begin with a sample of married contenders for promotion four years before the election in which some are promoted. Negative trend lines before this event reflect the fact that some relationships end in divorce each year. These trends do not differ between women and men who were subsequently promoted (solid black lines) and those who were not (dashed gray lines). These parallel trends end with the promotion event. The trend in remaining married takes a turn downward for promoted women relative to nonpromoted women, while promoted and nonpromoted men continue to have very similar paths.

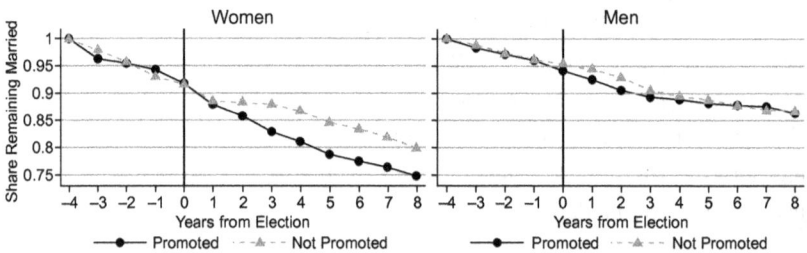

Figure 8 Trends in marriage durability for promoted and nonpromoted politicians.

Notes: The figure shows trends by event year in the proportion of politicians who remain married to their partner. The sample includes close contenders for promotion to mayor or parliamentarians who were married as of four years before the election in which they were a contender. N (Women) = 683, N (Men) = 1,556.

Causal Evidence for Promotion on Divorce

We estimate regression Equation (2) with OLS. Figure 9 plots the estimated gaps in the likelihood of remaining married for promoted and nonpromoted politicians. The graph on the left uses the time window starting four years before the election and ending eight years after. The one on the right restricts the window size for the pre-election period (politicians who were married as of one year before the election). This alternative specification produces the same results but expands our sample size substantially for the number of married people in the election year and for whom we can estimate the postelection effect on divorce. We therefore return to this specification in the more precision-demanding heterogeneity analysis in the section on mechanisms.

By examining the estimates for the pre-promotion years, $t = -4$, $t = -3$, $t = -2$, and $t = -1$, in the left graph we can verify the absence of preexisting differences in divorce trends between subsequently promoted and nonpromoted people. These estimates are small and lack statistical significance at conventional levels.

The results show large negative estimates in the postpromotion period ($t = 1$ to $t = 8$) for women but not for men. Women who were promoted are more likely to divorce afterwards compared to those who sought the same promotions but ultimately lost. Promoted women are 6 percentage points less likely

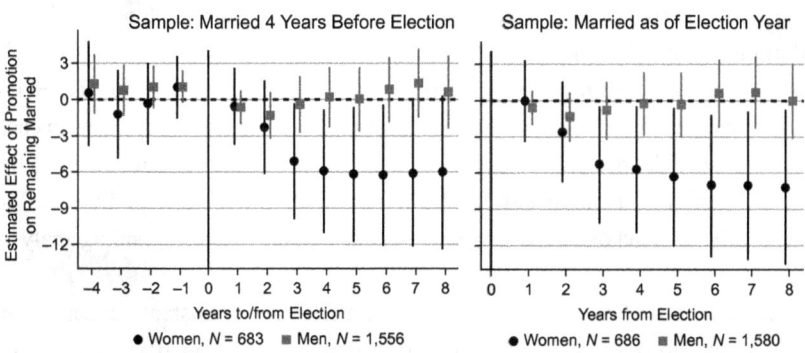

Figure 9 Effect of political promotions to mayor or parliamentarian on remaining married.

Notes: The figures show estimates from Equation (2) in separate samples for men (gray markers) and women (black markers). The markers show the percentage-point difference in the probability of remaining married between politicians who were promoted or not in each year compared to the baseline event year ($t = 0$). Vertical lines indicate 95 percent confidence intervals. The graph on the left uses a sample of promotion contenders who were married as of four years prior to the election ($t = -4$) and the one on the right uses a sample of politicians who were married as of the election year ($t = 0$).

to still be married at the end of their term in office than nonpromoted women, a 150 percent increase relative to the probability of divorce among nonpromoted women. The lack of a different pre-trend in divorce rates between these two groups makes it likely that women's divorces were caused by the promotion rather than by some other difference between the treatment and control groups.

Romantic Partner Support as a Mechanism

We have argued that women who have less career support from their romantic partner might incur more stress and strain on their relationship as they advance. Even if women politicians have the same time divisions in their households as their male counterparts, which is the case for nearly all top positions (recall Section 3), these divisions make women in politics stand out from the Swedish population. This fact may cause additional social strain on top of the role cycling and stressful bargaining situations (see West and Zimmerman, 1987; Akerlof and Kranton, 2000).

Section 3 examined if the division of paid and unpaid work could explain the career gap between men and women. Here we use the same approach to test whether the time divisions can explain the gender gap how promotions affect divorce rates. We directly test if gender differences in the share of household earnings can explain the gender gap in promotions in two steps. First, we estimate the gender gap in the treatment effect by interacting the treatment and time dummies with the female dummy in Equation (2) (we also interact all controls with the female dummy). In the second step, we add interactions for the politicians' share of household earnings. Comparing the estimated gender gaps in each event year with and without this control allows us to examine how much of the gender gap in the treatment effect can be explained by the earnings division. We lack sufficient data on temporary parental leave to run the corresponding analysis for that variable.

The black markers in Figure 10 indicate a clear and persistent gender gap in how promotions affect the likelihood of divorce. Four years after the election, the gender gap is 6 percentage points. The gray markers show that adding the interactions with the division of household earnings reduces the size of this estimated gender gap by about half. This suggests that the division of paid work within politicians' marriages is an important driver of the increased risk of divorce for promoted women relative to promoted men. Women whose career was already prioritized within their relationship before they were promoted experience a less intense shock to their relationship than women whose career was not the priority before promotion.

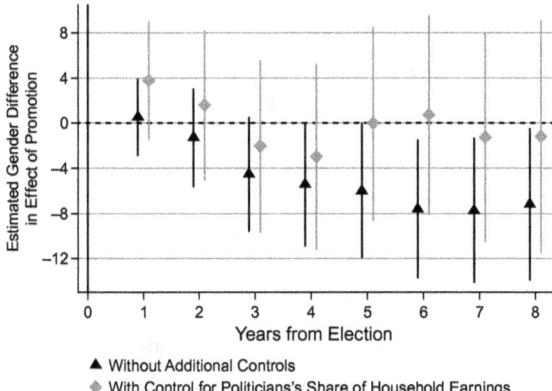

Figure 10 Romantic partner support and the gender gap in divorce after promotion.

Notes: The figure depicts estimates from regressions in which gender and the division of household earnings are added as interactions to all terms in Equation (2). The markers show the percentage-point gender gap in how promotions affect the probability of remaining married. Vertical lines denote 95 percent confidence intervals. The black markers show the estimates without controls for the division of household earnings and the gray markers show estimates from a model with the controls.

While we cannot include the division of parental leave as a control due to the multicollinearity issues discussed in Section 3, we can make the same type of split-sample analysis as in that section. We split the sample in the same way (according to whether the wife's share of the parental leave is below or above the median) and repeat the main analysis from Figure 9 in these two subsamples. While the estimates from this analysis are imprecise due to the small sample sizes, they clearly show that the divorce effect for women stems from the more traditional relationships rather than gender-equal ones (see Figure 11). In relationships where a promotion challenges the previous division of labor within the couple, the risk of divorce is higher.

7 Conclusions and Discussion: Where Do We Go Now?

In her pathbreaking book *The Politics of Presence*, Anne Phillips (1995) remarks how "in Athenian society, men were freed of domestic responsibilities by women and slaves, and were thus able to participate fully in the democratic process, a situation which is not dissimilar to the lives of many male politicians today." We provide new empirical evidence to demonstrate that romantic partnerships are still the source of substantial political inequality between women and men.

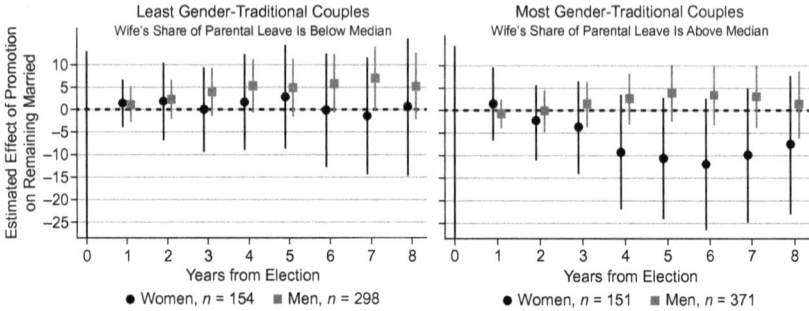

Figure 11 Difference in effect of political promotions on remaining married as a function of the division of parental leave.

Notes: The figures display estimates from Equation (2) in separate samples for men (gray markers) and women (black markers). The markers show the percentage-point difference in the probability of remaining married between politicians who were married as of the election year ($t = 0$) who were promoted or not in each year compared to baseline ($t = 0$). Vertical lines denote 95 percent confidence intervals. The graph on the left uses a sample of promotion contenders from couples in which the wife's share of parental leave was below the median (95 percent of the leave), and the graph to the right couples where it was above the median.

We analyzed detailed Swedish data to characterize time use patterns in politicians' romantic relationships. This description documented lower levels of career support for women politicians in terms of how their households split paid and unpaid work. Comparing politicians' relationships to those of the average Swedish household revealed an additional difference of interest: men in Swedish politics have a similar level of career support as men in the population, while women in politics differ starkly from women in the population. Women who climb to top political positions have considerably higher levels of career support than the average Swedish woman. This might offer a window into the potential social pressures on women politicians and their romantic partners as the woman's demanding political career requires the household to deviate far from the social norm.

We document large disadvantages for women in terms of re-election and political promotion in subnational politics. Women are less likely to accumulate seniority at the lower rungs of the political ladder, which makes them less likely to obtain leadership positions in their subnational party branches. We detected no gender gap in the likelihood of being promoted to parliament, and found that, compared to men with the same level of seniority in subnational politics, women were more likely to obtain a parliamentary seat—perhaps due to the greater transparency and affirmative action pressures for nominating candidates to parliament (discussed by, e.g., Johansson, 1999).[15] However, a freshman position in parliament is often less powerful than a top municipal position when the party heads the local government, and might best be characterized as a lateral or downward career move. In Johansson's (1999) study of the 1994 election, parties expecting to be the local incumbent saw it as more important to keep the "best" candidates locally.

Our analysis of women's re-election and promotion disadvantages in subnational politics supported our *Career support hypothesis*, which predicts that differences in career support from romantic partners help explain these disadvantages. Accounting for differences in how politicians divide paid and unpaid work in their relationships reduced the size of women's estimated disadvantages by 40–70 percent. This analysis also generated empirical evidence that a supportive romantic partner helps politicians advance. This evidence contributes to broader research on political ambition, career advancement, and family dynamics. Our analysis of high-coverage objective measurements of time allocations within households complements previous survey research on the role of romantic partners. Together with that work, our results suggest the utility of further research on romantic partners to understand gender inequalities in politics.

As in other careers, having a supportive romantic partner can help a person advance in politics. But extending our analysis to study parenthood demonstrated an important difference between sectors. While having children is a key factor in triggering expanded career inequalities in the labor market, this event is less important in politics. Political careers usually start alongside a person's regular job; transitions to full-time political jobs usually involve replacing the former private sector job with the political one. Thus most people have their children before entering politics. Our analysis demonstrated that this was the case and found no meaningful expansion of career gaps after having children, or an intensified role for partner support around this life event.

From a policy perspective, the lack of an important role for entering parenthood for women's career disadvantage reduces the impetus to provide parental leave or lactation rooms. A counterargument might be, of course, that such policies might encourage people to start their political careers earlier in life. The types of representatives who succeed in politics while their children are young, despite the lack of policy support (such as parental leave or lactation rooms), might be very different from other parents of young children and may not effectively represent their interests. For example, people who are encouraged

---

[15] During the period we study, local parties faced soft and hard quotas for elected positions in parliament. See Freidenvall (2005).

to enter politics because such support is available might have different policy priorities regarding public services such as childcare.

Finally, we studied how a lack of support from romantic partners can result in a high personal cost for women's political advancement. We compared the probability of divorce for women and men after receiving top promotions to parliament or mayor. The analysis supports our *Career stress hypothesis*, the idea that a lack of support from their romantic partner causes more stress and strain on women's romantic relationships as they advance in their political careers. We found that a top promotion doubled women's divorce rate but had no impact on the divorce rate for men. This analysis compares the relationships of close winners and losers for the same political promotion and thus has a strong causal claim.

The results for women's divorces provide valuable nuance to previous findings related to gender-equal promotion patterns from local to national politics. While women are not less likely to be elevated to these positions, they pay a larger personal price for their advancement. Given that divorce is usually the endpoint of a stressful dynamic within the relationship, this suggests women's work conditions are considerably worse than those of men. More women than men perform well at top political jobs *despite* their romantic partner, while more men than women perform well *because of* their partner's support.

To put the results into context, we calculate the promotion probabilities of men and women separately and examine the differences between partnered and single politicians. For men, the probability of promotion is substantially higher among politicians with a partner, but for women, having a partner makes no difference. For the average man's political career, a partner is a resource, but for the average woman's political career, a partner makes no difference. Since most politicians are partnered, and a partner is a resource only for men, it is not surprising that we observe a gender gap in the likelihood of promotion.

Discussions about romantic partners and gender equality in the labor market often focus on the importance of sharing household work more equally. Our research supports this argument but also demonstrates its limitations. People who advance to top positions in politics are not sharing equally: they have relationships in which both partners organize their time to favor the politician's career. This situation is likely a necessary consequence of the high demands on time and mental energy placed on people in top jobs. Put simply, if both partners held such jobs, they would never see each other or their children. Under these work conditions, a skewed pattern of time use may be unavoidable, which should shift the discussion from women and men sharing equally in each couple to women and men having the same distributions of time divisions. To advance in politics on an equal footing with men, women need the same access to a highly supportive relationship in which they have "married down" to a person willing to invest much of their time in the home front. Policy to facilitate these choices may need to address the strong social norms preventing most women and men from entering such relationships.

Future research on the gendered division of labor market and household work should examine the parity of support from husbands and wives. It remains uncertain whether we can perceive the role of a "partner" as equivalent across heterosexual men and women. For women aspiring to pursue a political career, having a partner who assumes roles traditionally associated with a wife is often essential. However, entrenched gender norms create distinct dynamics between having a stay-at-home husband versus a stay-at-home wife. The distribution of market and nonmarket work may also be affected. It is unclear whether a woman earning 60 percent of the household income holds the same bargaining position as a man in the same scenario.

We have interpreted the household division of labor mainly in terms of one partner's level of "career support" for the other. While this terminology is appropriate from the viewpoint that doing household labor constitutes the "ground service" for the other partner's career, it is less appropriate for capturing the well-being and life satisfaction obtained by doing (at least some of) those tasks. For example, building close and loving relationships with one's children can provide invaluable experiences that last a lifetime. An increased share of care work done by men would therefore not only help close the gender gap in careers but also give substantial added value to their (and their children's) lives. This perspective might help frame policy to further equalize household labor in already formed couples.

What types of government and organizational policies might help equalize women's and men's career outcomes and opportunities to perform well in their political positions? In the short term, policies might target the work requirements of political positions to make them easier to fulfil despite a lower level of partner support. This might include making the political job more flexible (e.g., facilitating telework or part-time work) or introducing policies that help shorten the workweek or divide positions between more individuals. In the medium term, policies might help reduce the amount of unpaid household work by providing, for example, low-cost and accessible childcare and elder care. They could also directly target time divisions via policy provisions such as individual earmarks in parental leave programs. Long-term policies should undoubtedly address couple formation.

References

Akerlof, G. A., & Kranton, R. E. (2000). Economics and identity. *Quarterly Journal of Economics*, **115**, 715–53.

Allen, P. (2013). Gendered candidate emergence in Britain: Why are more women councillors not becoming MPs? *Politics*, **33**(3), 147–59.

Almås, I., Kotsadam, A., Moen, E. R., & Røed, K. (2023). The economics of hypergamy. *Journal of Human Resources*, **58**(1), 260–81.

Amato, P. R. (2010). Research on divorce: Continuing trends and new developments. *Journal of Marriage and Family*, **72**(3), 650–66.

Angelov, N., Johansson, P., & Lindahl, E. (2016). Parenthood and the gender gap in pay. *Journal of Labor Economics*, **34**(3), 545–79.

Anzia, S. F., & Bernhard, R. (2022). Gender stereotyping and the electoral success of women candidates: New evidence from local elections in the United States. *British Journal of Political Science*, **52**(4), 1544–63.

Azmat, G., Hensvik, L., & Rosenqvist, O. (2022). Workplace presenteeism, job substitutability and gender inequality. *Journal of Human Resources*, **58**(1), 1121-12014R2.

Becker, G. S. (1973). A theory of marriage: Part I. *Journal of Political Economy*, **81**(4), 813–46.

Becker, G. S. (1974). A theory of marriage: Part II. *Journal of Political Economy*, **82**(2), S11–S26.

Becker, G. S. (1981). *A Treatise on the Family*. Cambridge, MA: Harvard University Press.

Becker G. S., Landes, E. M., & Michael, R. T. (1977). An economic analysis of marital instability. *Journal of Political Economy*, **85**, 1141–87.

Bernhard, R., Shames, S., & Teele, D. L. (2021). To emerge? Breadwinning, motherhood, and women's decisions to run for office. *American Political Science Review*, **115**(2), 379–94.

Besley, T. (2006). *Principled Agents? The Political Economy of Good Government*. Oxford: Oxford University Press.

Besley, T., Folke, O., Persson, T., & Rickne, J. (2017). Gender quotas and the crisis of the mediocre man: Theory and evidence from Sweden. *The American Economic Review*, **107**(8), 2204–42.

Bittman, M., England, P., Sayer, L., Folbre, N., & Matheson, G. (2003). When does gender trump money? Bargaining and time in household work. *American Journal of Sociology*, **109**(1), 186–214.

References

Bledsoe, T., & Herring, M. (1990). Victims of circumstances: Women in pursuit of political office. *American Political Science Review*, **84**(1), 213–23.

Bonica, A. (2020). Why are there so many lawyers in Congress? *Legislative Studies Quarterly*, **45**(2), 253–89.

Bos, A. L., Greenlee, J. S., Holman, M. R., Oxley, Z. M., & Lay, J. C. (2022). This one's for the boys: How gendered political socialization limits girls' political ambition and interest. *American Political Science Review*, **116**(2), 484–501.

Boschini, A., Hakansson, C., Rosén, A., & Sjogren, A. (2011). Trading off or having it all? Completed fertility and mid-career earnings of Swedish men and women. Institute for Labour Market Policy Evaluation Working Paper.

Brady, H. E., Verba, S., & Schlozman, K. L. (1995). Beyond SES: A resource model of political participation. *American Political Science Review*, **89**(2), 271–94.

Budig, M. J., & England, P. (2001). The wage penalty for motherhood. *American Sociological Review*, **66**(2), 204–25.

Burns, N., Schlozman, K. L., & Verba, S. (2001). *The Private Roots of Public Action: Gender, Equality, and Political Participation*. Cambridge, MA: Harvard University Press.

Campbell, R., & Childs, S. (2014). Parents in parliament: "Where's mum?" *The Political Quarterly*, **85**(4), 487–92.

Carroll, S. J., & Sanbonmatsu, K. (2013). *More Women Can Run: Gender and Pathways to the State Legislatures*. Oxford: Oxford University Press.

Cirone, A., Cox, G. W., & Fiva, J. H. (2021). Seniority-based nominations and political careers. *American Political Science Review*, **115**(1), 234–51.

Cotta, M., & Best, H. (2007). *Democratic Representation in Europe: Diversity, Change, and Convergence*. Oxford: Oxford University Press.

Coverman, S. (1989). Role overload, role conflict, and stress: Addressing consequences of multiple role demands. *Social Forces*, **67**(4), 965–82.

Craig, L., Powell, A., & Smyth, C. (2014). Towards intensive parenting? *The British Journal of Sociology*, **65**, 555–79.

Crowder-Meyer, M. (2020). Baker, bus driver, babysitter, candidate? Revealing the gendered development of political ambition among ordinary Americans. *Political Behavior*, **42**(2), 359–84.

Dal Bó, E. D., Finan, F., Folke, O., Persson, T., & Rickne, J. (2023). Economic and social outsiders but political insiders: Sweden's populist radical right. *The Review of Economic Studies*, **90**(2), 675–706.

Dodson, D. L. (1997). Change and continuity in the relationship between private responsibilities and public officeholding: The more things change, the more they stay the same. *Policy Studies Journal*, **25**(4), 569–84.

Eagly, A. H. (1987). *Sex Differences in Social Behavior: A Social-Role Interpretation*. Hillsdale: Lawrence Erlbaum.

Eagly, A. H., & Wood, W. (2012). Social role theory. In P. A. M. Van Lange, A. W. Kruglanski, & E. T. Higgins, eds., *Handbook of Theories of Social Psychology*. England: Sage, pp. 458–476.

Eggers, A., & Jens Hainmueller. (2009). MPs for sale? Returns to office in postwar British politics. *American Political Science Review*, **103**, 513–33.

Ekberg, J., Eriksson, R., & Friebel, G. (2013). Parental leave – A policy evaluation of the Swedish "Daddy-Month" reform. *Journal of Public Economics*, **97**, 131–43.

Ely, R. J., Stone, P., & Ammerman, C. (2014). Rethink what you "know" about high-achieving women. *Harvard Business Review*, **92**(12), 101–109.

England, P., Bearak, J., Budig, M. J., & Hodges, M. J. (2016). Do highly paid, highly skilled women experience the largest motherhood penalty? *American Sociological Review*, **81**(6), 1161–89.

Eriksson, R., & Nermo, M. (2010). Care for sick children as a proxy for gender equality in the family. *Social Indicators Research*, **97**, 341–56.

Esteve-Volart, B., & Bagues, M. (2012). Are women pawns in the political game? Evidence from elections to the Spanish Senate. *Journal of Public Economics*, **96**(3–4), 387–99.

Folke, O., Persson, T., & Rickne, J. (2016). The primary effect: Preference votes and political promotions. *American Political Science Review*, **110**(3), 559–78.

Folke, O., & Rickne, J. (2016). The glass ceiling in politics: Formalization and empirical tests. *Comparative Political Studies*, **49**(5), 567–99.

Folke, O., & Rickne, J. (2020). All the single ladies: Job promotions and the durability of marriage. *American Economic Journal: Applied Economics*, **12**(1), 260–87.

Fox, R. L., & Lawless, J. L. (2010). If only they'd ask: Gender, recruitment, and political ambition. *The Journal of Politics*, **72**(2), 310–26.

Fox, R. L., & Lawless, J. L. (2014). Reconciling family roles with political ambition: The new normal for women in twenty-first century US politics. *The Journal of Politics*, **76**(2), 398–414.

Fransson, S. (2018). Vinna eller försvinna?: De politiska nätverkens betydelse i kampen om en plats i riksdagen (Doctoral dissertation, Linnaeus University Press).

Freidenvall, L. (2005). Kvinnors väg in i politiken (Women's pathways into Swedish politics) Rapport presenterad vid Vi är många, vi är hälften – ett seminarium om kvinnor i politiken. Jämställdhetspolitiska utredningen, Regeringskansliet.

Fulton, S. A., Maestas, C. D., Maisel, L. S., & Stone, W. J. (2006). The sense of a woman: Gender, ambition, and the decision to run for Congress. *Political Research Quarterly*, **59**(2), 235–48.

Goldin, C. (2014). A grand gender convergence: Its last chapter. *American Economic Review*, **104**(4), 1091–19.

Goldin, C., & Katz, L. F. (2011). The cost of workplace flexibility for high-powered professionals. *The Annals of the American Academy of Political and Social Science*, **638**(1), 45–67.

Grumbach, J. M., Sahn, A., & Staszak, S. (2020). Gender, race, and intersectionality in campaign finance. *Political Behavior*, 1–22.

Hideg, I., Krstic, A., Trau, R. N. C., & Zarina, T. (2018). The unintended consequences of maternity leaves: How agency interventions mitigate the negative effects of longer legislated maternity leaves. *Journal of Applied Psychology*, **103**(10), 1155–64.

Hochschild, A. (1989/2003). *The Second Shift*. New York: Avon Book.

Hsieh, C. T., Hurst, E., Jones, C. I., & Klenow, P. J. (2019). The allocation of talent and US economic growth. *Econometrica*, **87**(5), 1439–74.

Ichino, A., Olsson, M., Petrongolo, B., & Thoursie, P. S. (2023). Taxes, childcare, and gender identity norms. Working Paper.

Iversen, T., & Rosenbluth, F. (2006). The political economy of gender: Explaining cross-national variation in the gender division of labor and the gender voting gap. *American Journal of Political Science*, **50**(1), 1–19.

Johansson, J. (1999). *Hur blir man riksdagsledamot? En undersökning av makt och inflytande i partiernas nomineringsprocesser*. Stockholm: Gidlunds förlag.

Johansson, E. A. (2010). The effect of own and spousal parental leave on earnings (No. 2010: 4). Working paper.

Jonsson, L. (2003). Kommunstyrelseordförande: Kommunledare med politisk förankring (Municipal Council Board Chair: Municipal Leader with a Political Mandate). Västra Frölunda: Nya Doxa.

Joshi, D. K., & Goehrung, R. (2021). Mothers and fathers in parliament: MP parental status and family gaps from a global perspective. *Parliamentary Affairs*, **74**(2), 296–313.

Kitroeff, N., & Silver-Greenberg, J. (2018). Pregnancy discrimination is rampant inside America's biggest companies. *New York Times*, June 15.

Kleven, H., Landais, C., Posch, J., Steinhauer, A., & Zweimüller, J. (2019). Child penalties across countries: Evidence and explanations. *AEA Papers and Proceedings*, **109**, 122–26.

Kotakorpi, K., Poutvaara, P., & Terviö, M. (2017). Returns to office in national and local politics: A bootstrap method and evidence from Finland. *The Journal of Law, Economics, and Organization*, **33**(3), 413–42.

Kotsadam, A., & Finseraas, H. (2011). The state intervenes in the battle of the sexes: Causal effects of paternity leave. *Social Science Research*, **40**(6), 1611–22.

Krook, M. L. (2010). *Quotas for Women in Politics: Gender and Candidate Selection Reform Worldwide*. Oxford: Oxford University Press.

Krook, M. L., & Mackay, F. (eds.). (2011). *Gender, Politics and Institutions: Towards a Feminist Institutionalism* (Vol. 1). Basingstoke: Palgrave Macmillan.

Lundberg, S., & Pollak, R. A. (1993). Separate spheres bargaining and the marriage market. *Journal of Political Economy*, **101**(6), 988–1010.

Lundberg, S., & Rose, E. (2000). Parenthood and the earnings of married men and women. *Labour Economics*, **7**(6), 689–710.

Maestas, C. D., Fulton, S., Maisel, L. S., & Stone, W. J. (2006). When to risk it? Institutions, ambitions, and the decision to run for the U.S. House. *American Political Science Review*, **100**(2), 195–208.

Nilsson, T. (2001). Den lokalpolitiska karriären: En socialpsykologisk studie av 20 kommunalråd (The Local Political Career: A Social Psychology Study of 20 Full-Time Local Politicians). PhD Thesis, Växjö University.

Niven, D. (1998). Party elites and women candidates: The shape of bias. *Women & Politics*, **19**(2), 57–80.

Norris, P., & Lovenduski, J. (1995). *Political Recruitment: Gender, Race and Class in the British Parliament*. Cambridge: Cambridge University Press.

O'Brien, D. Z., & Rickne, J. (2016). Gender quotas and women's political leadership. *American Political Science Review*, **110**(1), 112–26.

Ohlsson, B. (2017). Duktiga flickors revansch. Bokförlaget Forum. Stockholm.

Palmer, B., & Simon, D. (2003). Political ambition and women in the US House of Representatives, 1916–2000. *Political Research Quarterly*, **56**(2), 127–38.

Palmieri, S. (2018). Gender-sensitive parliaments. In W. R. Thompson, ed., *Oxford Research Encyclopedia of Politics*. Oxford: Oxford University Press. https://oxfordre-com.ezproxy.ub.gu.se/politics/view/10.1093/acrefore/9780190228637.001.0001/acrefore-9780190228637-e-215.

Phillips, A. (1995). *The Politics of Presence*. Oxford: Oxford University Press.

Prillaman, S. A. (2023). *The Patriarchal Political Order: The Making and Unravelling of the Gendered Participation Gap in India*. New York: Cambridge University Press.

Reich-Stiebert, N., Froehlich, L., & Voltmer, J. B. (2023). Gendered mental labor: A systematic literature review on the cognitive dimension of unpaid work within the household and childcare. *Sex Roles*, **88**, 1–20.

Reid, M. G. (1934). *Economics of Household Production*. New York: Wiley.

Sapiro, V. (1982). Private costs of public commitments or public costs of private commitments? Family roles versus political ambition. *American Journal of Political Science*, **26**, 265–79.

Schein, V. E. (1973). The relationship between sex role stereotypes and requisite management characteristics. *Journal of Applied Psychology*, **57**(2), 95–100.

Schein, V. E., Mueller, R., Lituchy, T., & Liu, J. (1996). Think manager – think male: A global phenomenon? *Journal of Organizational Behavior*, **17**(1), 33–41.

Teele, D. L., Kalla, J., & Rosenbluth, F. (2018). The ties that double bind: Social roles and women's underrepresentation in politics. *American Political Science Review*, **112**(3), 525–41.

Thomas, M., & Bittner, A. (eds.). (2017). *Mothers and Others: The Role of Parenthood in Politics*. Vancouver: UBC Press.

Thomas, M., & Bodet, M. A. (2013). Sacrificial lambs, women candidates, and district competitiveness in Canada. *Electoral Studies*, **32**(1), 153–66.

Thomsen, D. M., & King, A. S. (2020). Women's representation and the gendered pipeline to power. *American Political Science Review*, **114**(4), 989–1000.

UNDP (2023). Breaking down gender biases: Shifting social norms towards gender equality. 2023 Gender Social Norms Index Report. https://hdr.undp.org/system/files/documents/hdp-document/gsni202303pdf.pdf.

van Dijk, R. E. (2023). Playing by the rules? The formal and informal rules of candidate selection. *Women's Studies International Forum*, **96**(5), 102669. https://doi.org/10.1016/j.wsif.2022.102669.

Verba, S., & Nie, N. (1972). *Participation in America: Political Democracy and Social Equality*. New York: Harper and Row.

Weeks, A. C. (2022). The political consequences of the mental load. Working Paper.

Weiss, Y., & Willis, R. J. (1997). Match quality, new information, and marital dissolution. *Journal of Labor Economics*, **15**(1), S293–S329.

West, C., & Zimmerman, D. H. (1987). Doing gender. *Gender & Society*, **1**(2), 125–51.

Widenstjerna, T. (2020). Vem väljer vem och varför?: Om betydelsen av homosocialitet och personliga kontakter i partiers nomineringsprocesser. PhD thesis. Mid Sweden University.

Wylie, K. N. (2018). *Party Institutionalization and Women's Representation in Democratic Brazil*. Cambridge: Cambridge University Press.

Cambridge Elements ≡

Gender and Politics

Tiffany D. Barnes
University of Texas at Austin

Tiffany D. Barnes is Professor of Political Science at the University of Texas at Austin. She is the author of *Women, Politics, and Power: A Global Perspective* (Rowman & Littlefield, 2007) and, award-winning, *Gendering Legislative Behavior* (Cambridge University Press, 2016). Her research has been funded by the National Science Foundation (NSF) and recognized with numerous awards. Barnes is the former president of the Midwest Women's Caucus and founder and director of the Empirical Study of Gender (EGEN) network.

Diana Z. O'Brien
Washington University in St. Louis

Diana Z. O'Brien is the Bela Kornitzer Distinguished Professor of Political Science at Washington University in St. Louis. She specializes in the causes and consequences of women's political representation. Her award-winning research has been supported by the NSF and published in leading political science journals. O'Brien has also served as a Fulbright Visiting Professor, an associate editor at *Politics & Gender*, the president of the Midwest Women's Caucus, and a founding member of the EGEN network.

About the Series

From campaigns and elections to policymaking and political conflict, gender pervades every facet of politics. Elements in Gender and Politics features carefully theorized, empirically rigorous scholarship on gender and politics. The Elements both offer new perspectives on foundational questions in the field and identify and address emerging research areas.

Cambridge Elements

Gender and Politics

Elements in the Series

In Love and at War: Marriage in Non-state Armed Groups
Hilary Matfess

Counter-Stereotypes and Attitudes Toward Gender and LGBTQ Equality
Jae-Hee Jung and Margit Tavits

The Politics of Bathroom Access and Exclusion in the United States
Sara Chatfield

Women, Gender, and Rebel Governance during Civil Wars
Meredith Maloof Loken

Abortion Attitudes and Polarization in the American Electorate
Erin C. Cassese, Heather L. Ondercin and Jordan Randall

Gender, Ethnicity, and Intersectionality in Cabinets: Asia and Europe in Comparative Perspective
Amy H. Liu, Roman Hlatky, Keith Padraic Chew, Eoin L. Power, Sam Selsky, Betty Compton and Meiying Xu

Gendered Jobs and Local Leaders: Women, Work, and the Pipeline to Local Political Office
Rachel Bernhard and Mirya R. Holman

What's Happened to the Gender Gap in Political Activity? Social Structure, Politics, and Participation in the United States
Shauna L. Shames, Sara Morell, Ashley Jardina, Kay Lehman Schlozman and Nancy Burns

Glass Ceilings, Glass Cliffs, and Quicksands: Gendered Party Leadership in Parliamentary Systems
Andrea S. Aldrich and Zeynep Somer-Topcu

Family Matters: How Romantic Partners Shape Politicians' Careers
Johanna Rickne, Olle Folke and Moa Frödin Gruneau

A full series listing is available at: www.cambridge.org/EGAP